LIVING
THE FREELIFE

A Step by Step Guide to Overcoming
Bullying, Abuse, and Living the Life of
Your Dreams

BROOKE DEBOER

For more information, email thebrookedeboer@gmail.com.

ISBN: 979-8-9899783-0-4 - paperback

ISBN: 979-8-9899783-1-1 - ebook

ISBN: 979-8-9899783-2-8 - hardcover

ISBN: 979-8-9899783-3-5 - audobook

Get Your Free Gift!

To get the best experience with this book, I've found readers who download and use my *Living the FreeLife* Reflection Exercises are able to implement changes faster and take the next steps needed to heal from bullying and abuse and become confident again!

You can get a copy by visiting:
https://thebrookedeboer.com/author/

I dedicate this book to my sweet husband, Derek, and my three beautiful daughters, whom I love with all my heart. If I can help them avoid some of the pain of my experience and live the lives God has intended for them, I have done what I need to do here.

FOREWORD

In "Living the FreeLife," Brooke DeBoer shares a narrative that's deeply aligned with the transformative power of facing our truths and forging a path to freedom. Her journey echoes a universal struggle against the shadows of adversity. Brooke's story is a testament to the resilience of the human spirit, showcasing her entrepreneurial approach to life—not in business, but in redefining success and guiding others to do the same.

Her spiritual quest for a higher purpose mirrors the challenges we all face. Brooke's solutions, rooted in self-discovery and authenticity, offer hope and direction. This book is more than a memoir; it's a lifeline for those seeking to reclaim their lives from the past's grip.

As you turn the pages of "Living the FreeLife," let Brooke's story inspire you to break free from your limitations and strive for a world that reflects the beauty of your dreams. Her masterclass in transformation is a mirror to our collective potential to change, love, and heal.

Embrace Brooke DeBoer's courageous journey, and may it inspire you to embark on your own path of healing, growth, and ultimate freedom.

Ryan Blair
#1 NYT Bestselling Author
CEO AlterCall

PREFACE
TO MY FUTURE LIGHTS
OF THE WORLD

*When we long for a life without difficulties, remind us
that oaks grow strong and diamonds are made under
pressure.*
Peter Marshall

Recently, I was in Africa, speaking to my new friend Sam, a Maasai warrior. We could feel his loving nature and joy from the moment we met him. The way we were treated in Africa changed me. My daughters were visibly moved by how we were treated and cared for. He asked, "Why does America have such a high incidence of suicide and mental health problems?"

I told him, "There are many angry and sad people, and many feel alone even if they are successful."

He looked at me with sadness and then told me with sincere kindness that he cared to help the situation. I have yet to work with him, but I hope to bring him to America to share and spread his joy. I often say that I left part of my heart in Africa, and that's true, but what I am committing to do now is to be courageous enough to tell my story and bring back the part of my heart that was filled in Africa by the genuine kindness of people we barely knew. We still speak to those friends almost daily.

After four months of writing my story, I felt stuck. Everything was mechanical, and I was just going through the motions to follow my outline for the book. I was doing that thing I've learned to do after being bullied at many points in my life, powering through, going through the motions, being strong, and swallowing the tears. Showing that no matter what I have felt or experienced, I still could be strong and accomplish something. But that's not what I wanted the book to be about. So, I started over.

I will lay it all out here in this book, and it will be the most therapeutic and courageous thing I have ever done. For years, I have heard the message, "You should write your story." It would regularly and often come through and then immediately be followed with all the limiting beliefs about why I shouldn't and what negative things could result from this kind of vulnerability. When I heard that, the next messages were:

Why would you do that? Put it all out there for everyone to criticize!?

Why would you make yourself uncomfortable like that?

Who do you think you are to share your story? It's not that bad!

Are you a victim? You've done bad things, too.

Why should you tell how people hurt you? You've hurt others!

Why do you think you deserve this kind of attention? Remember when you ran for office in high school, and you lost? No one wants you to lead them in anything!

As I write this, tears well up in my eyes, and I get that feeling I've felt time and time again of resisting the cry, the lump-in-the-throat feeling, attempting to swallow the tears and suck it up. You know it, the one where your throat feels tight as you push the expression back down, swallowing it, hoping the feeling goes away. My new thing is, if I feel like crying, I'm going to practice letting it out.

I'm sharing all of it because this is what I want you to do. I want you to be free of what you've stored inside for so long; I want those tears to come out and fall down your cheeks. I want you to be free to share your emotions when they come and learn how to process the pain and let it go. I want you to be all you can be, and until you are free of the anger and the sadness, you are not free. I want you to be free of pain, heaviness, and criticism. I hope by the end of this book, you are blooming like a flower, slowly opening to life again, open to receiving love, warmth, and kindness, and sending them back out into the world. I want you to know that nothing that happens to you is your fault or something you must carry forever. I want you to feel peace, love, and light. I want you to know your worth!

This book is also for those who have bullied someone or mistreated someone. Understand that bullying has many forms. I hope this wakes you up to realize that your spot in the puzzle, masterpiece, or whatever metaphor you want to use is also important. When you mistreat people, you have the potential to be part of snuffing out their light, which creates more holes in the big picture. What good is a puzzle with a bunch of missing pieces? The pieces that remain don't get to shine with a bunch of pieces missing; it all looks incomplete. If we truly are all connected, as I believe we are, what happens to one of us happens to all of us.

EFFECTS OF BULLYING

I just saw a beautiful post on Instagram by an influencer, BC Serna.[1] He shared a story of when he was bullied and what

---

1   BC Serna, Instagram, accessed November 1, 2023, https://www.instagram.com/bc_serna/.

he started hiding as a result. Someone made fun of his teeth, so he didn't smile for ten years (showing his teeth) afterward. As he shared his story, he got choked up. I could feel his pain like it was my own. It touched me so much that he was putting it out there so vulnerably and cared so deeply about reaching others who may have gone through this experience. It gave me the courage to share my whole story, not just the parts proving that I've overcome and have it all together, but all of it.

I wrote this book for everyone who has been told they are not good enough. This is for anyone who has been left out, told to be quiet, to change who they are, stepped on, run over, or made fun of. It's okay to stand up for who you are. It's okay to ask for something you need. It's okay to take up space and let your light shine. God created you for a purpose that only you can fulfill. If you don't do it, there will be a missing piece in humanity's grand puzzle, a hole designed to be filled so we can't see the entire picture.

Even though I've been bullied at almost every stage of my experience to various degrees and developed different coping mechanisms (some rather destructive over the years), I have always believed that I have a part in making the world a happier place. I often think about some of the first times someone was mean to me and how shocking it was. I was reminded of this the other day when my daughter came home from work, and I could tell she was holding onto something hard. She was busily walking around the kitchen, getting a snack, and began sharing with me what happened at work that day.

She had just started a new job; this was day two, and as she shared, I could see her holding back the tears. She had been on the phone with a customer who was frustrated about something, and as she went to hang up the phone, the guy said, "Go f*ck yourself." As she told me this, and I held space for her to share and offered a hug, the tears came. My heart broke a little at that moment because I realized this was her first experience with a complete stranger being so harsh and mean. The world can be so cruel sometimes. Each time, it takes a piece of our innocence away, and we learn to fight, hide, or heal from it.

My mom experienced a trauma when I was a young child, and our family was given no choice but to move through it and heal; it took many years. I didn't even know how I carried that until I was an adult. Girls who were jealous and mean bullied me in elementary school, middle school, and high school. Even some mothers the girls I was friends with were saying terrible things in group settings about me. Much of what I've seen with my girls seems to stem from parents living through their kids and behaving like their kids or worse, by gossiping and disparaging young people to elevate their kids or make themselves feel better.

In my adult life, I've been specifically left out of women's friend groups, not given grace or an opportunity to resolve issues with friends, shunned, or talked about behind my back. It was hurtful to learn that people were saying terrible things about me that others couldn't even bring themselves to repeat, because it was so nasty. My girls have been specifically left out of social groups at school suddenly and without explanation. I think those are the most hurtful because, for a responsible person who cares about learning and growing and being a good person, you are not given an opportunity to resolve issues, leaving you feeling confused, alone, and sad.

ARE YOU UNCOMFORTABLE?

At this point, you are likely uncomfortable because you know you've done this to people, or you are feeling sadness now with me, or perhaps some anger. Anger is a secondary emotion; there is always something underneath. It took me a long time to learn that. I am sharing all this to have the tough conversation about bullying and its effects. I want to acknowledge those who have been through it and hopefully jar the ones who have dished it out to consider a different way. I say that with so much love because I know people shut you out, mistreat you, and say terrible things about you because they feel that way about themselves. Let's face it: hurt people, hurt people.

I also believe that no baby comes into this world with a mean bone in its body. I believe we are all children of God, and when we go out into the world, we have experiences that knock us around, and we choose to respond or react. Most of us do this unconsciously until we learn better ways. Through this process, we can develop hard edges, defense mechanisms, a strength that pushes us into perpetual motion, or grief that sends us inside ourselves, snuffing out our light and keeping us from sharing our gifts with the world.

FINDING HEALING FROM BULLYING

However you have learned to cope with your pain, I hope to help you find ways to acknowledge your hurt or behavior if you are dishing it out. I hope to provide you with some tools and ideas about how you can move forward and heal. I aim to inspire you to serve and complete the puzzle of life by helping you find forgiveness for yourself and others. Each one of us is a puzzle piece in one grand puzzle, and not one of us is the same for a reason. The frame of the puzzle needs every piece to complete the picture. To create the structure, we need the centerpieces, too, all of you! We each have a role to play and something we can do to complete it.

Recently, I chose my role with plenty of intentional work, work that I plan to share with you in this book. One of my coaches asked me to create an alter ego, a state that I wanted to live in. She asked me to think about the strongest, most empowered version of me, to call it up and describe to her how it felt, what color it was, what my body was doing when I felt that way, and what I was telling myself. I worked through this little exercise with her, and the color was a golden light. My body was sitting up, chest forward, with a smile on my face. I was radiating light out into the world, and I felt strong. I call her "Sunshine Fierce." Most of us are going through the motions, surviving and reacting to the world around us. I learned from this coach that I was the creator of my experience, and I get to be the creator of my life story. I am an active participant, and where I place my energy and intention is what I manifest. This can be your experience, too.

I hope to inspire you to be resilient and keep going, to find your strength, truth, and light to share it with the world. There will be resistance to your healing. As you stand for your worth and work on your growth, a chemicalization will happen. Things will bubble to the surface; you'll be forced to deal with them, but God gives you the strength and everything you need to do the work.

My friend just posted a quote, "Your light is going to aggravate a lot of unhealed people. Glow anyway, sis," a further reminder that it's important to let your light shine! You are a gardener planting seeds. Envision the garden you want to create. Imagine the seeds you are planting. As Tony Robbins says, "Where focus goes, energy flows,"[2] just like watering and feeding a garden. If you feed anger, jealousy, negativity, and unforgiveness, that grows. If you feed your garden love, light, kindness, and lift and serve others, this will grow.

---

2   Team Tony, "Energy Flows Where Attention GOES - Focus & Energy: Tony Robbins," tonyrobbins.com, September 8, 2022, https://www.tonyrobbins.com/career-business/where-focus-goes-energy-flows/.

As the Bible says in **Psalm 128:**

[1] Blessed are all who fear the LORD, who walk in his ways. [2] You will eat the fruit of your labor; blessings and prosperity will be yours.

[3] Your wife will be like a fruitful vine within your house; your sons will be like olive shoots around your table. [4] Thus is the man blessed who fears the LORD.

[5] May the LORD bless you from Zion all the days of your life; may you see the prosperity of Jerusalem, [6] and may you live to see your children's children. Peace be upon Israel (Psalm 128:1–6).

I hope to help you grow a tree that produces life, love, happiness, and peace. Without light on the issue of bullying, it cannot heal. I am sending you so much love and strength in your healing process.

XO,
Brooke, aka Sunshine Fierce

TABLE OF CONTENTS

PHOTOS

CHAPTER 1

LOOKING IN THE MIRROR

One can never consent to creep when one feels an impulse to soar.
Helen Keller

I was lying in bed, feeling nauseous and alone. I reached for my Bible and held on for what felt like dear life. My mom had asked me if I was ready to be a mom the night before. We discussed options because this was not the plan. My dad shared with me later how he felt when I called to tell them I was pregnant. With his voice strained, he said, "When you called, I felt like I got kicked in the stomach." I know this was not the way they hoped things would go for me.

I was dating the father of my baby. I wouldn't call it dating, however. Dating had all but disappeared in this day and age. He was my boss at a local restaurant near where I was finishing college in Florida. I had just graduated from college, and my dream was to go to Los Angeles and work in the film industry. When I received the news, it wasn't surprising, but I could feel my dreams slipping away. The timing wasn't what I had planned, but it's hard to say there really was a plan upon looking back at the situation. One of my dreams was to become a mom. I knew I would be a good one, but it wasn't supposed to happen now. I had things I wanted and needed to do to grow up and discover my purpose. I guess God had other plans, partly assisted by some marginal choices on my part, and I could feel the heavy weight of the responsibility.

Winter Park, where I had been living in Florida, was a beautiful place with glimmers of the life I desired to live. It was sunny and warm; the seven lakes surrounding the area were connected, and the homes were beautiful. Somewhere inside of me, I envisioned a beautiful life ahead, but it was as if I was in a dark room peering at the cracks of light coming through. I realized I didn't have a plan, and life felt like it was happening *to* me.

I had one friend who stayed close to me, and the man I was dating had pushed her almost entirely out of the picture. I took part in this outcome. I had moved in with him and was spending less and less time with my friends and more with him. The distractions of the often tumultuous relationship even had me worried about going to see Oliver Stone speak at the University of Central Florida. We would argue a lot, and he didn't mesh with the other parts of my life. There was a significant age difference of ten years, which played a part in him not having an interest in my friends or my college experience.

I had tickets to see Oliver Stone, one filmmaker I looked to for inspiration, as my dream was to make movies, but I had become so isolated from friends, and he wasn't supportive of my interests. My life was slowly becoming wrapped around his interests and family. I chose to go hear Mr. Stone speak despite his resistance and my isolation, which turned out to be an excellent decision amongst many questionable ones. It helped me keep a speck of my dream alive. I remember how inspired I felt hearing Stone speak that day, and I came back with a little extra skip in my step, which quickly was tripped up by the life I had unconsciously been creating with him.

Even on the first date, I felt something was off. As my teenage daughter now says, "Did you get the ick, Mom?"

I'd have to say I had the ick in moments, but there was something that kept me with him. I pushed past this feeling and went on a date. He was handsome and older. Maybe there was something about him being in the next phase of life that was attractive to me. I still occasionally strive to find what held me there. I was driven but lacked a plan, so I went with the feelings.

The relationship had its good moments, but looking back, I see that most things were not a fit. The family lifestyle differed greatly from my own. He liked to smoke weed, and I wasn't into that, so he would hide it from me. We couldn't connect on faith because he wasn't into going to church, and I wasn't exactly pushing to go, either. He worked at a restaurant, and I had dreams of going to Hollywood. I liked to run and work out, but he didn't. I wasn't fond of his friends and didn't trust them. But I was just living and experiencing life and not thinking too far into the future until a horrible thing happened, and it left me wondering what hit me.

All I remember is the sneers of laughter coming from the house as I hit the ground outside a party I had asked not to go to. We were out at a bar watching baseball; it was playoff time. We had some drinks, and then he said he wanted to go to our co-worker's party. I didn't trust or like this co-worker after an experience I had after a night of partying with him and one of his friends. I was nervous, in fact, to go to the party, as I had a bad experience with two of the guys who were there. Sam drove there anyway, and our argument escalated as we drove. He was essentially mocking me and completely ignoring my concerns. I became more non-compliant and anxious as we drove until I outright refused to go to the party. We were still arguing when we got there. He parked the car. I got out to challenge him one last time about going in, and he refused to listen.

I am amazed that he could completely ignore my obvious distress and push me to go. I hissed, "You can't make me go in there; I want to go home!" He fiercely grabbed my forearms, and when I attempted to break free, he threw me on the ground. I landed on my left shoulder in a heap. In shock, I quickly realized there was no remorse as he was walking away toward the party.

I could hear laughter coming from the house where the party was. He left me lying in the street, unable to move. The shooting pain in my shoulder became very intense, and I realized I could hardly move. There was a brief pause where everything felt like slow motion, and I literally said to myself, "Oh, no, now what will I do?"

Moments later, I saw headlights and a car driving into the cul-de-sac toward me. A college-age guy with dark hair got out of his car and asked me if I needed help. All my usual safety concerns went out the window. I was like a broken-winged bird lying helpless. I surrendered, and he gently picked me up off the street and asked me what had happened. I told him I was thrown to the ground and I didn't know what to do. He offered to take me to his house, and sadly, this was a better option than going back to the party to ask for help from my "so-called" friends.

I'm not sure if I prayed; I had almost entirely pushed God out of my life during this time. The only important thing was keeping this relationship alive, which obviously was not working. Miraculously, my rescuer's mom was a nurse. He said we could call his mom and ask her to check my injuries out, and we could figure out what to do.

I believe in angels and that God provides us with protection even when we don't ask for it; it was all I had at that moment. Clearly, the people I thought were at least acquaintances were not my friends. They didn't care about me. My favorite Bible story growing up was the story of the Good Samaritan, who stopped by the side of the road to help the man.[3] I was fortunate that this "angel," my Good Samaritan, came to my aid. I wish I could remember his name now to thank him.

Once we got to his apartment, the pain intensified; I was confused, hurt, embarrassed, and ashamed. I felt numb, but there was one distraction. He had a bathtub full of tiny kittens. I had always had cats. One adopted our family and had kittens on my dad's office shelf when we were kids, and I begged him to keep them. We kept one baby, appropriately named Baby Kitty, and the mama. Fluffy and Cottonball were their official names; I know they were so creative! Ha! They effectively became Baby and Mama.

When I was a teenager, a friend and I saved a kitten from the middle of the road, a tiny gray- and white-striped kitten with green eyes. Smokey became my best friend until I left for college. He liked to sleep right on my head and cuddled all the time. I believed cats were little messengers in my life, part of that little glimmer of light that would show up from time to time for many years before I realized I could let the light in myself. Healing takes time.

WHEN LIFE IS HAPPENING TO YOU

I like people, so I usually can find some things that I like about anyone. I like to look for goodness. Sometimes, I was very blind to the things that weren't good for me, or I would choose to ignore the internal messages I would get warning me that something wasn't right. I was just wandering through life, being led from moment to moment by how I felt, like a leaf blowing in the wind. I had other experiences in college where I was influenced to make decisions inconsistent with my values. Even if I didn't want a relationship, I would sometimes agree to date a person and then not feel good

---

3   Luke 10:25–37.

afterward. The partying, combined with my inability to make clear boundaries for myself and not having the confidence to stand for my values, pushed me into some emotionally confusing situations. Again, there wasn't a plan for how these decisions or situations would play out in the future.

I knew many young women who were sexually assaulted in college in various situations. I remember a friend confiding in me about a night of drinking and partying at the nearby university, and how she was taken advantage of while intoxicated. Another friend, who really struggled with self-esteem, was hooking up with many guys, while intoxicated, who didn't respect her or want a relationship with her. I was worried about my friends; however, it would have been healthier to be more focused on my well-being. It is always easier to worry about others than to slow down and look at our own hearts. This would have required being quiet, taking the time to examine my own decisions, why I was making them, and how they had affected my heart.

One harrowing experience was a night when we were hanging out at our apartment and pool. Some friends from work came over for drinks, and I have no memory of that night after the first couple of drinks. I woke up partially undressed and with broken glass from a fallen picture off my bathroom wall. Still, to this day, I have a bad feeling about what happened there. I have no memory of it and fear the worst. I was not prone to blacking out or drinking to that level, and I never did drugs. I tried weed only twice in high school, and it didn't work for me. I felt very paranoid and was relieved I could remove that pressure.

All these experiences felt like life was happening to me. When I was thrown to the ground and blacked out on the night at my apartment, I knew these were not a result of my choice, but choices were leading up to them that could have shifted the outcome. The question was, why wasn't I strong enough to make better relationship choices? I knew the difference between right and wrong, but I didn't know that I didn't have to wait for things to happen to me.

LIFE-CHANGING MOMENTS

After my friend came to get me from my Good Samaritan angel helper, the entire hot mess that I was, I felt numb. My heart was hurting, I was scared, and my shoulder was very painful and could not be moved. I didn't want to go to the hospital. I wanted to forget that it had even happened, which seemed to be a pattern that I was developing with these experiences. I spent several days at my friend's house, where she took care of me and helped me with things. I couldn't move my left arm, so she had to cut my food for me. I felt pathetic and lost, and I didn't want to tell my parents. I knew I didn't feel safe getting my things from Sam's alone, so I was encouraged to call the police. What semblance of strength I had left picked up the phone and dialed the non-emergency line. They sent an officer out to meet with me at Melinda's front door.

He explained to me that Florida is a zero-tolerance state for domestic abuse and that for him to help me, I would need to agree to press charges. I didn't want to do it, but I reluctantly agreed. The thought immediately flashed in my mind, "What would they do?" I felt like I was up against the world with his two protective sisters, and I was still taking responsibility for what had happened. My head was a mess. One minute, I was angry and felt like I wanted to fight for my freedom, and the next, I felt totally responsible for the situation escalating to where I was thrown to the ground. The officer took one look at me and my five-foot frame and asked me how tall my boyfriend was. I told him, "Over six feet."

He said, "You are a small person; there's no chance that anything you did warranted him throwing you on the ground and causing you to be hurt in this way."

His authoritative and clear support was a moment of truth that planted a seed of confidence in me. Unfortunately, the guilt and shame overrode this boost, and I soon ignored his supportive advice.

The police notified Sam that I would be pressing charges and obtained a key to the apartment. The officer escorted me to the apartment, and I retrieved all my belongings. The rest is kind of blurry after that. I received phone calls from Sam's sister asking me not to press charges. They were pushy and unsympathetic, defending their brother.

Within a short time, I succumbed to the pressure, agreed to drop the charges, and began seeing him again. The emotional attachment and fear of being alone overrode the warnings coming from everyone else who cared about me. Shortly after that, I felt different and wondered if I might be pregnant. Sure enough, I took a pregnancy test, and it was positive.

I laid the test in his bathroom on the back of the toilet and shared the news with him. Sam was ten years older than me and not even close to what I wanted in a man, but I didn't know I could even ask for what I wanted. I didn't even know what I wanted. Inside, I had some ideas, but no one had ever talked to me about what I wanted my future to look like or what kind of husband I was looking for. I didn't know how to write the qualities and values of the person and that I could ask for what I dreamed of. I was just living and going toward where I got attention and what I was attracted to at the moment. My life was totally upside down.

Later that day, Sam's family came over to the house. His brother-in-law went to the bathroom, found the pregnancy test, brought it out into the living room, and said, "What's this?" I should have been more careful, but who does that? This man had no boundaries, not a thought about how this would make anyone feel. I'm sure they already didn't like me based on the history of our relationship, but I wanted to crawl into a hole and die. I was so embarrassed! These people had no boundaries, no class, and no sensitivity.

I got this incredible impulse to run, another glimmer of hope amidst an increasingly dark situation. All I wanted to do was go home to Oregon. I got the courage to call my parents and felt a determination to overcome this hole I had dug myself into. It was this night that I found the little strength I had buried under all the shame to tell Sam I wanted to go home and that I was going with or without him. He agreed to drive to Oregon with me. He was very attached to his family, so at some level, I knew this would not be the best plan, but I didn't care. I had a drive to feel safe and knew things had gone terribly wrong, but I did not know how to fix it. His family was intensely pressuring him to stay. They couldn't understand why he would uproot his life for me. I stood strong like an oak tree, and it remains one of my proudest moments amongst a heap of shame.

I had made so many poor decisions at this point, and I had realized that there was no repairing the damage if I continued my current course. I would have to change the trajectory of where I was headed. I insisted on going home, and shortly after that, we began driving across the country. The things I had tolerated before with Sam slowly became intolerable. I realized on the drive, staying in crappy hotels along the way, that this was not at all the future I had envisioned as a younger girl. Sam smoked cigarettes, and suddenly, I couldn't stand the smell of him. I felt completely emotionally disconnected from him. I felt like I was living an out-of-body experience in a foreign country; it was like a nightmare I wasn't waking up from. Nothing felt normal or right, and I was extremely uncomfortable.

As I headed home, I focused on my good, loving family; even then, they were supporting me, letting me stay with them until I figured things out. I was always independent, wanting to forge my own path, and the life I had created in

Florida differed from how I was raised. I really had myself in a mess this time. There was no way out but through, and I knew that, so I committed to making it right by becoming the best mom I could be. I was going to have this baby, and I would figure out how to be a mom. I had occasional glimmers of a beautiful life, including being a mom someday, being in love with an amazing, kind husband, and living well in a pretty home even while going through this dark time. The romance I had envisioned, however, was slipping away. Now I know I didn't really have it in the first place. I had just hoped that's what it was.

LISTEN TO YOUR INNER VOICE

Once I got home to my parents, I struggled even to get out of bed. I was hurting but trying to survive and be strong at the same time. My daughter was another angel coming into my experience to help redirect me. Paige was the new angel visitor, and I had to become strong for her. I was broken down and had forgotten my worth, so having someone else do it for me was helpful. I began piecing my life back together, trying to make sense of what I was feeling. Sam had come with me to Oregon to attempt a life together and asked me to marry him, and I had agreed. He stayed with my parents as well. Before even driving back to Oregon, I had lined up a job. I didn't tell them right away that I was pregnant, but I let the company I had worked for in Oregon know I was coming home, and they made a place for me.

After several days of working at my new job, pushing through the morning sickness, I learned while I was at work, Sam was sleeping in and not looking for work. Everything felt wrong. I didn't feel proud to introduce him to my friends in Oregon. I knew he was not right, but I hadn't admitted that out loud, and part of me felt like I needed to make it work since he was the father of my child. One of my friends from high school met him and shared with me she didn't think this was a match. She was tactful but honest.

One night, we went downtown to one of my family's favorite restaurants to look at it as an option for a rehearsal dinner. My mom had brought one of her friends, and we were having appetizers at the bar. It was Lebanese, and the food was amazing! But Sam didn't like it. He made it known and spent the entire time criticizing the food and making comments about how weird the place was. It was almost like an undisciplined child with awful manners. I was four months pregnant, going through bodily changes, and feeling just over the hump on morning sickness, so I had a lot going on. Sitting there, I could feel my heart rate increasing and the anger boiling up in me from all his comments. I excused myself to go to the bathroom to try to contain my emotions. I found myself in front of the mirror in the bathroom with tears streaming down my face. I looked in the mirror and said, "I'm done. I can't do this!" I felt a full conviction about what I needed to do. My true self was coming through, my guide. I'm thankful, to this day, that I listened.

I wiped my tears, walked out of the bathroom, and told Sam to meet me outside the restaurant. I heard myself say, with almost no reaction and no need for anything to be said to fix it, "I'm done, and I don't care if I ever f*cking see you again." And I meant it! I was done being treated badly. I was done being the one to fix it. I was done with the dark. I wanted to find the light. I knew my daughter could be part of that, even though I was terrified of becoming a mom and doing it alone. I felt like God was calling me to lift my standards and open myself to more potential. I did not know what that would take or how I got to this point, but I knew one thing: I likely had the determination to figure it out. This was the hope for a new beginning.

MASLOW'S HIERARCHY OF NEEDS

There's some excellent research to help you understand where you are in your healing process and why you feel the way you do. Once I became a coach, many things became clearer with the tools that were provided. One such tool is Maslow's Hierarchy of needs.

HIERARCHY OF NEEDS

the 5 basic human needs

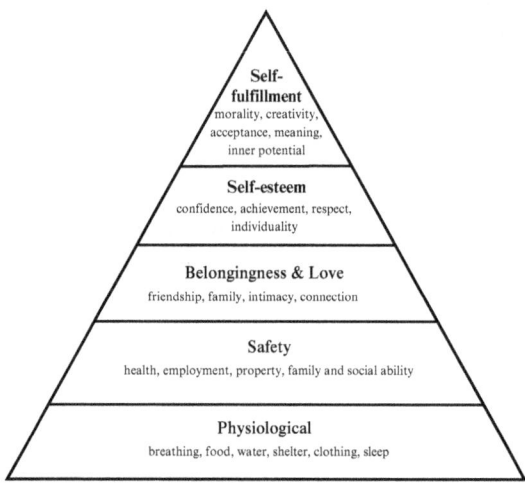

Years later, when I became a coach, I understood why I kept choosing relationships that weren't healthy. According to Maslow, your needs will be met in order, starting with your basic physical needs all the way up to self-actualization. If the needs of safety and security, love and belonging, and self-esteem are not met, it will be impossible for you to grow in morality and experience purpose and inner potential. If you struggle with health issues, for example, it makes it more challenging to be employed and socialize. If you aren't employed and don't have your health, spending time on friendships and intimacy where we get a sense of connection becomes difficult.

It's hard to develop your self-esteem if you are not feeling a sense of love and belonging, safety and security, and your physiological needs are not being met. I struggled with safety after hearing about my mom's trauma and not being able to make sense of how she could be hurt in this way. Another child may not have taken it in so much, but for me, it created an awareness of the potential dangers out there in the world, and I had a hard time knowing what to do with that.

So, to move from safety and security to love, belonging, and intimacy, we need to feel safe and understand that we have our basic needs met. Then, we can move toward building our self-esteem and confidence. If you are not feeling safe, it is important that you ask for help to get to a safe place. Surround yourself with safe people who can support your growth.

If you are in an unsafe home or relationship and need help, there are several organizations and hotlines you can contact for guidance and support. These organizations provide resources, counseling, and assistance in various situations of abuse or unsafe environments. See Appendix B for more information.

It's challenging to access trauma sometimes, especially if it happened to us when we were young enough and unable to process it. In my case, a lot happened in my teen years, which I will address in an upcoming chapter, that eroded my self-confidence and reduced my ability to keep a standard for myself. I was aware of it but in survival mode and did not know how to unpack it, let alone heal it. I journaled to express my feelings, prayed, and eventually got therapy to talk through what had happened and learn about healthy relationships and boundaries.

Here are some various ways to understand the trauma you have experienced. None of these are better than any other. Do what works for you. Sometimes, it's essential to try different things until you find your answers.

1. Cognitive processing therapy (CPT) is a common therapy option for healing trauma.
2. Prolonged exposure therapy.
3. EMDR.
4. Somatic Experiencing (SE™)
5. Certain types of talk therapy.
6. A movement practice.
7. Journaling to understand the impact of trauma and your emotions.

I share my story with you from a healed perspective. From time to time, my fight-or-flight mechanism kicks in when I feel I'm being dominated in a conversation. Other times include when I'm presented with a communication challenge with a person who doesn't respect me as an individual with my own thoughts. This response comes from being literally pushed around and dominated in unsafe relationships in my past.

For those of you who have experienced any trauma from bullying, abuse, relationships that lack respect, or any other situation that would make you feel unsafe, it's important to know that there is help for you! You can learn to unpack the trauma and, like peeling back the layers of an onion, heal your story one piece, one layer at a time. I have spent many years praying, in therapy, and doing personal reflection work to become the person I want to be. I still slip up from time to time, but I am so much more at peace having done the work! It is worth it.

I'm here to help guide you to do the work of understanding your heart and being honest about your story and journey so that you can heal. You've got this!

WHAT I'VE LEARNED

Everyone who wills can hear the inner voice. It is within everyone.
Mahatma Gandhi

I had so many chances to listen to my inner voice through all that and many other experiences in my life, and I didn't. Looking back to examine why I didn't is interesting. Most of the time, I was scared to change how something was going for fear of the unknown, or I really thought I wanted whatever was happening. I was attached to specific outcomes, and I didn't have a plan. When they say hindsight is 20/20, it's really the truth!

Now I know things I didn't know then, so some of it happened because I just didn't know any better. A lot of it happened because I was afraid, and I wanted to feel loved. I believe my inner voice and God were speaking to me the entire time. At some level, I knew my worth, and I knew I deserved a safe love, but it was buried under a pile of painful memories that stacked up over time. These memories act like scar tissue. It creates a little hardness each time you feel emotionally wounded. After a while, you feel rigid, and it becomes harder and harder to see your worth.

When Sam came to go on our first date, something inside me said, "I don't know." I felt unsure if the attraction was there and a general reservation, but I pushed past it, ignoring my inner voice. I wouldn't change having my daughter for the world. She has taught me more about myself than most of my other life lessons and mistakes. She is not a mistake but a blessing, and I wouldn't be who I am today without her and without the experience of having to figure out how to listen to my intuition, love myself, and be a good role model for another precious living being.

I had other times as a kid when I heard a voice guiding me. Often, I wouldn't listen, but sometimes I did. As a younger school-aged child, it was about being accepted by my peers. Once, as a teenager, I got into a car where some girls had been drinking, and we crashed into a ditch. We were all fortunate to survive. I knew I should have said "no," but I didn't. We've all probably done things we know we should not do, pushing past the warning signs, but the voice and protective presence are always there if we can listen for and heed it.

The biggest lesson I've learned is to listen to my inner voice. After several miserable relationships, big mistakes, and almost 50 years of living and raising my girls, I can say that the practice of listening to your intuition is invaluable. Not only will it save you so much heartache down the road, but it will be a guide for you, creating an easier, more peaceful path to where you are going and who you are growing into.

What You Can Do

One of my favorite childhood authors, Shel Silverstein, wrote a poem about how only you can determine what is right for you.[4]

> There is a voice inside of you,
> That whispers all day long,
> "I feel that this is right for me,
> I know that this is wrong."
> No teacher, preacher, parent, friend,
> Or wise man can decide,
> What's right for you—Just listen to

---

4   Shel Silverstein, "The Voice."

the voice that speaks inside.

Intuition is instinct. It is the ability to understand something immediately, with no conscious reasoning. When we get in our head, we snuff out the inner voice. It becomes hard to hear once we justify the behavior we are doing after we hear the message. We hear our inner voice when we feel emotions like fear and anxiety, but also physical sensations— like feeling tense and persistent thoughts, dreams, and suspicions. My parents used to tell me that when I feel harmony and peace, it is the time to decide. If you are having mixed emotions, feel confused, or tense, that's your intuition asking you to pause and get clear.

One of the most overlooked signals of intuition is confusion. As the author of *Self-Care for Empaths,* Tanya Carroll Richardson, says, "It's that wise part of you that can float high above the details of the moment, your own emotions, and the emotions of others to get an eagle-eye, more objective perspective on a situation."[5] When we are in a hurry, forcing things to move forward, or just simply not taking the time to be by ourselves to get clear, we can often push past the inner voice speaking. Allowing for quiet moments can help you connect to this intuition or inner knowing.

As a Christian, what helped me is the Scripture: "Be still and know that I am God."[6] In the stillness, we find our voice, we hear our truth, and we can transform ourselves into who we were originally intended to be without the noise of the world, other people's opinions, or our own emotional confusion that arises from being disconnected from our true voice.

---

5   Tanya Carroll Richardson, *Self-Care for Empaths: 100 Activities to Help You Relax, Recharge, and Rebalance Your Life* (New York, NY: Adams Media, 2020).
6   Psalm 46:10.

If you didn't listen, you still have angels to guide you through. Don't beat yourself up! It might be a bumpy ride, but the angels will keep you safe. You may have to work your way back or to a new situation, but you'll get there.

REFLECTION QUESTIONS

To begin your healing process, let's start with some journaling and reflection questions about your life, what you've been through, and how it made you feel. Once we connect to our feelings, we can work on healing them and improving the connection to our inner voice and intuition. To help you understand the trauma you've been through, here are some reflection questions for you to work through to help you take the first step of acknowledging it. Trauma healing isn't just about processing your uncomfortable feelings but also about post-traumatic growth. Many people find journaling a useful (and healthy) tool to cope with trauma, and so can you. If you've experienced a traumatic event in your life, then using journaling as a healing tool can help you come to terms with it and learn how the trauma has affected your life.

Combining journaling with psychotherapy can also help speed up your trauma healing. If you've experienced trauma in your life, then it is recommended that you speak to a professional counselor or therapist for support and guidance.

Connecting with a therapist can help you learn to process the emotions trauma brings and cope with unpleasant emotions and feelings.

1. Do you believe that your trauma is holding you back from moving forward in life? Write about how it makes you feel.
2. How can you show yourself the same understanding, compassion, and kindness as you would your loved one?
3. What ways do you still have healing to do?

4. What five things, people, or places make you feel safer?
5. What ways have you persevered despite the trauma you've experienced?
6. What fears have you had as a child, teenager, and adult? How have you coped with them?
7. How was it when you were growing up? Was your childhood home stable or abusive?
8. Write about the relationship between your parents and yourself. How has their influence impacted your life?
9. What is one thing you wish your loved one understood about you?
10. What event triggers your fight-or-flight response the most?
11. What kind of support did you need when you were growing up but felt you did not receive?

Action Step: Relationship Trauma Quiz

Answer the following questions with "Yes" or "No."

1. Have you ever experienced repeated verbal or physical abuse from a family member, partner, or peer during your childhood or adulthood?
2. Do you frequently feel anxious, fearful, or on edge in your relationships, even when there is no apparent threat?
3. Have you ever felt controlled or manipulated by someone who made you feel powerless?
4. Do you struggle to trust others in your relationships due to past experiences of betrayal or deceit?
5. Have you ever had difficulty setting healthy boundaries with friends or partners, resulting in feelings of being taken advantage of or being too accommodating?

6. Do you experience flashbacks or intrusive memories related to past abusive or bullying relationships?
7. Are you inclined to avoid close relationships or social situations due to fear or discomfort stemming from past experiences?
8. Have you noticed changes in your self-esteem or self-worth because of past abusive or bullying relationships?
9. Do you frequently ruminate on negative experiences or relationships, finding it difficult to let go of past events?
10. Do you feel a sense of detachment or emotional numbness about your current relationships?

Scoring:

Count the number of "Yes" responses. The higher the number of affirmative answers, the greater the likelihood of having experienced relationship trauma associated with bullying and abuse. If you have concerns about the impact of these experiences on your mental health and well-being, it is advisable to seek professional guidance and support.

CHAPTER 2

CONNECTING TO YOUR VALUES

Living into our values means that we do more than
profess our values; we practice them.
Brené Brown in *Dare to Lead*

A s I reached out to God and spent a lot of time asking myself questions about how I got where I was, it also forced me to really dig deep and find my values. I had strayed for quite some time from what my true values were, moved away from attending church or reaching out to God in prayer, and disconnected from friends and family because all my energy was going toward trying to make this relationship work. I lived with a constant feeling of insecurity and a nagging sense that something really was not right. Just by being in something that wasn't working, I could connect to some of my values. For example, before we moved from Florida to Oregon, I learned he was lying to me about things he was doing. Because of the trust being broken, I discovered I value honesty in a relationship.

One thing I knew was that I wanted to be a good mom; I wanted to provide for my daughter, and I wanted her to have a sense of family. Sam wasn't getting up to find work while staying with my parents, so I could see what that might look like. I had already secured a job and was on a path to build my career and be able to support myself. I grew up working with my dad and always had a job. I knew I wanted a partner who was at least working as hard as I was. Here, I learned other things I value: work ethic and having a partner who is a teammate who works as hard as I do. There was more focused work to be done, but this pushed me to start the work and listen to what my heart wanted instead of listening to everyone else and putting my feelings and values on the back burner.

One thing I learned the most from was planning to become a parent. Preparing to become a mom has been a profound journey of self-discovery, during which I've learned and honed my core values. As I contemplated the immense responsibility of nurturing and raising a child, I found my values became clear guides for the path ahead. The importance of love, compassion, and patience became evident as I realized these qualities would be the cornerstones of my parenting. Balancing work and family life illuminated my values concerning ambition, success, and the significance of a harmonious work-life equilibrium. The commitment to my child's education underscored my value for continuous learning and knowledge. Moreover, fostering a sense of community and building a robust support system revealed the significance of relationships in my life.

This transformative journey of preparing for motherhood has been a catalyst for introspection, allowing me to recognize and strengthen the values I hold dearest and carry them forward as a parent, shaping the way I navigate the world and inspiring my child to do the same.

If you have been abused or mistreated in unhealthy relationships, you too can decide right now to change the trajectory of your life. Embracing humility, practicing honesty about your situation, and breaking free from unhealthy attachments in relationships are fundamental steps toward reclaiming one's life after enduring abuse or bullying. By humbly acknowledging that no one deserves mistreatment, you empower yourself to seek healing and growth. Honesty about your experiences opens the door to receiving support, whether from loved ones or professionals, and allows you to release the weight of secrecy and shame.

Recognizing and breaking free from unhealthy attachments is liberating, as it clears the path to self-discovery and fosters relationships built on mutual respect and genuine care. These pivotal actions not only restore self-worth but also serve as a transformative process for changing the course of life, enabling survivors to emerge stronger, more resilient, and with a newfound sense of purpose and inner strength.

FINDING HUMILITY

True humility is not thinking less of yourself; it is thinking of yourself less.
C.S. Lewis

I wanted to find humility and release my desire to control my experience humanly and let God lead me and ask for the help and support of loved ones. As I did, I found strength. I knew I had made a lot of mistakes trying to force relationships to work, change people, and hang on to things that weren't for me. I was allowing the fear of the unknown to overrule my ability to make sound choices consistent with my values. After Sam left, I knew I had a tough road ahead, but I had no choice but to put one foot forward and get started. If I had thought about it too much, I wouldn't have made it. I knew I needed just to move ahead. I prayed a lot, and my prayers weren't very sophisticated. They were, "Please, God, help me have the strength to get through this and to become a good mom," and "Dear God, I am ready to be healed of the past and walk in the path you would have me walk." I asked myself what I wanted more of in my experience, and I slowly thought again about the love and life I wanted.

I moved into an apartment as part of my new job in management. I could begin my life again and get a fresh start. My parents helped me set up Paige's room. My church held a baby shower for me. I struggled with shame and feeling like I didn't deserve it, but I let them in, and they showed me unconditional love. I began planning for when I had to go back to work, what I would do for Paige's care. I found a woman from church to watch after her. I could feel God's presence amid this challenge, bringing me the people I needed for the support and love I needed to continue.

HONESTY

The human mind always wants to push away the uncomfortable. Repeating patterns in our lives often comes from not wanting to be honest with ourselves, because the truth is painful. It requires us to be uncomfortable, and nobody likes to feel that! When I looked in the mirror and told myself, "No more of this!" with Sam, that was the moment the pattern broke. Our motivation to change is because we know there is pleasure in changing and moving toward our dreams and goals or because we are in so much pain and realize that if we don't change, it can only get worse. This was where I was at. In a course called Unleash Her Power Within with Karissa Kouchis, I learned that sometimes it's important to be brutally honest with ourselves, and that equals clarity.[7] When we can be honest about who we are now and who we want to be and get a picture of the gap in between, it is the moment we have an opportunity to change. We understand we are not where we want to be. Without this honesty and

---

7   Karissa Kouchis, "Unleash Her Power Within – Powered by Tony Robbins," accessed December 7, 2023, https://uhpw.com/.

willingness to be uncomfortable, we have little chance to grow.

SETTING BOUNDARIES AND RECOGNIZING UNHEALTHY ATTACHMENTS

When I was fifteen, I fell in love with a boy who had a lot of trauma and problems. He was adopted at age five and remembered his blood brothers and mom. He vividly remembered the day he was given up. He then went to foster home after foster home until he landed at one with a seemingly normal family. The older foster sister in the home was involved in beauty pageants and was very beautiful. She was the biological daughter of the family, and the boy was the foster child they took in. When he acted up, he was locked in the garage and made to eat dog food. One day, the foster dad broke his arm. Years later, he had the scars to prove it—a constant reminder of the abuse.

After hearing all these stories, I thought I could save him. I threw everything I had into helping him feel good about life and the current adoptive family he was living with. I took it on as my responsibility. He had a good heart and was kind to me. He wanted to be with me and gave me a lot of attention. He made me feel like I was the most important thing in the world to him, until he couldn't accept the love he got in return, and then he sabotaged it by doing drugs and running away with a wild older kid.

When he would run away, I would become despondent and depressed. I was on a roller coaster ride of emotions. I spent most of my time waiting for him to come back and tell me he loved me and that everything was okay. I couldn't make sense of why he would betray me and disrespect his adoptive family. Finally, my parents had to step in and say "no" to me seeing him. It was affecting my moods, my social life, the way I treated my family, and my grades. When we are younger and even sometimes when we are older, we can't see what is at work in our own relationships because we are attached to the person and the idea of what we are hoping the relationship is and will be.

Setting boundaries amid an attachment to a potentially unhealthy relationship can be a challenging but crucial step toward self-preservation and personal growth. It begins with self-reflection and recognizing the importance of self-care. Start by identifying the specific behaviors or dynamics that are causing you distress or harm within the relationship. Once you have clarity, communicate your boundaries clearly and assertively, emphasizing that they are not negotiable. Remember that boundaries are about protecting your well-being and asserting your values. Be consistent in enforcing these boundaries, even if it means creating some distance in the relationship.

Seek support from trusted friends, family, or a therapist to help reinforce your boundaries and provide emotional guidance during this arduous process. Ultimately, setting and maintaining boundaries in an unhealthy relationship is an act of self-love and a crucial step toward achieving a healthier and more balanced life.

What I've Learned

It's really important to stand up for yourself and not always agree with what people say if indeed you don't feel that that's true.
Lily Collins

I had not been good at setting my boundaries. Growing up, I was always influenced by strong personalities because of my strong desire to be liked. I couldn't stand the feeling of being left out or pointed out. I just so badly wanted to fit in and be liked. What I didn't understand then was that I was trading my peace to please others, and this is a very natural human desire. We all want to be seen and loved. The problem is when we go out into the world, and for some of us, even in our own families, not everyone has our best interests at heart. It may not even be a conscious choice by those around us to hurt us, but it happens because of years of their own dysfunction. Regardless, it is up to us to understand our values, have the humility to listen to Divine guidance, and get clear on our boundaries. Brene Brown defines boundaries simply as "What is okay and what is not okay with us."[8] I didn't have any idea that this was something I needed to know. I was just going through life doing things for unconscious reasons, mostly to receive love.

With Sam, communicating my boundaries the first time he disregarded my concerns about something would have been helpful, and then having the strength not to worry about his response and stand up for myself if he disagreed. It didn't start with him throwing me on the ground. It started with him flirting with and having secrets with one of our co-workers and lying to me about smoking weed and so on. At one point, I borrowed his car and brought my dog along, and the dog ate an entire bag of marijuana that was stored under his driver's seat. He didn't tell me it was in there. I could have been pulled over and arrested, or the dog could have died. Looking back, I realize this story even seems a bit humorous as it is so outside of what would be acceptable to me today. This happened early in the relationship, and I just kept going. Setting boundaries early is essential, and I should have ended it then. I didn't really understand the importance of this or even understand what boundaries were.

Recently, I've been watching the lawyer show *Suits*. The main character, Harvey Specter, played a pivotal role in helping Mike Ross disconnect from his unhealthy

---

8   Brené Brown, *Rising Strong* (San Francisco, CA: Instaread, 2015).

relationship with Trevor. Specter kept telling Mike Ross that he needed to disconnect from this friend. He was dealing drugs and getting into trouble with the law, and even set him up to deliver drugs. Once he was hired at Harvey's law firm, Harvey's mentorship and unwavering belief in Mike's potential served as a catalyst for personal growth. He provided Mike with a healthier, more constructive connection and a positive role model, which contrasted with Trevor's self-destructive tendencies.

By offering him an opportunity to work at a prestigious law firm, Harvey not only empowered Mike with a fresh start but also guided him toward a more productive and fulfilling path. He helped him see the importance of setting firm boundaries and choosing who we let into our lives. This transformation reflected the importance of surrounding oneself with positive influences and mentors to break free from harmful relationships and pursue a better future. More on mentors later!

WHAT YOU CAN DO

The process is simple: identify your core values, turn them into specific behaviors, and then use them to create your life and serve as a catalyst for genuine change. Like most things in life, it's simple but not easy. If you are feeling confused, unconfident, and really lost, check in with your values. Allow yourself some time to look honestly at what your values are and write them down. If you need help to identify your values, see Appendix A.

When someone shows you who they are, believe them the first time.
Maya Angelou, American author and poet

Sometimes we are attached to helping someone, and we can't see how it is negatively affecting us. This is why it's so important to know what your values are; put those first, and then, if it works and fits with your values, you can add someone else in.

When someone you are with is emotionally unstable, controlling, abusive, or generally unkind, it is up to you to teach them how to treat you. And do you know how you do that? You do it by what behavior you accept. I finally learned this as an adult when I was processing everything with a therapist. She sent me a video by Brene Brown explaining setting boundaries in very simple terms.[9] It finally clicked. She describes it as being generous toward others while continuing to lead with integrity and staying true to yourself. Setting boundaries means prioritizing your needs and practicing self-care without feeling guilty.

If you find yourself amid a scary change, you can also reach out to God or whatever higher power you believe in for guidance. The humility that is required will give you a sense of peace as you practice it. To surrender is the ultimate relaxation exercise. Take your thoughts about your problem and yourself and perhaps the pain you are feeling, and try giving it to God. Ask for the way to be shown to you and for a sense of direction. At first, it likely will not feel like it, but as you do it, it will bring you an increased awareness of your attachments either to a person or an outcome. This, in turn, brings a new perspective with which you can view your predicament.

Boundaries are best when they are made early and often. If you haven't made any boundaries yet, it's okay. Every day, every minute, is a chance for a fresh start!

---

9   First Aid Arts, "Boundaries with Brene Brown," Vimeo, September 27, 2023, https://vimeo.com/274228723.

Reflection Questions

To help you determine what boundaries you need to create, here are some reflection questions to help you understand where your relationships are and what may need to change.

1. Do you and your partner challenge each other to be better?
2. Do your friends and family think that your relationship has long-term potential?
3. Do you and your partner accept each other for who you truly are?
4. Do you share the same core values? What are your core values?
5. Do you get along with your partner's family?
6. Do you both feel secure in the relationship?
7. Are you team players in your relationship?
8. Do you respect each other? Does he/she respect you?

Action Step: Identify Your Values

- Look at Appendix A for a list of values or, in the Additional Resources section of this book, you can also find a link to view Brene Brown's value list in her book, *Dare to Lead,* as a helpful resource to identify your specific values. Make a list of your top three to five values and reflect on how they are showing up in your life now.

Chapter 3

HOW DID I GET HERE?

*Life is divided into three terms - that which was,
which is, and which will be. Let us learn from the past
to profit by the present, and from the present, to live
better in the future.*
William Wordsworth

I started my parenting journey with no clue of what I was doing. I honestly don't know how you do something this hard without God. I reached out to God with a humble heart and asked Him or Her to lead. I consider God as our Father and Mother, encompassing all the qualities: eternal, all-knowing, all-seeing, and all-wise. I figured I had screwed things up enough that I was ready to be led. Once we get to this point, we get ourselves out of the way, and it allows God to go to work. I believe God is always working, but if we are busy undoing or not seeing the work that is happening, we are missing the messages, teaching, and guidance God is sending.

[12] Yet to all who did receive him, to those who believed in his name, he gave the right to become children of God— [13] children born not of natural descent, nor of

31

human decision or a husband's will, but born of God (John 1:12–13).

If God is our parent, then I reasoned He wouldn't leave me high and dry, even if I had made mistakes, and that I could be forgiven. I knew the answers would come, but it was so scary not to know what was coming. I went about learning to be a parent. It was just Paige and me in our little apartment. I had a little help with childcare when I needed to go back to work. I believe it was an answered prayer. The result of making a mature decision to find employment also helped me create a home since I had a paid-for apartment through maternity leave. Knowing I would have to support us on a single-parent income, I began saving as soon as Sam left, so I would have enough to get through maternity leave.

I went back to work after three months. This was excruciating for me. Paige and I had really bonded, and I really loved being a mom, however challenging. It was difficult in so many ways, but I loved it. The bond between a mother and child is so incredible! Friends came to visit me, and some friends stood by me. The reactions from family and friends were not as awful as I thought they would be. I had a new focus now, so it didn't really matter, anyway. Once I had Paige, I had a new gauge for what I wanted to be part of or not.

LEARNED BEHAVIORS

Shortly after I started back at work, I got a call from my high school friend, Molly, saying a guy I had met in college, Derek, was asking about me and heard I had moved back to Oregon. I asked her what he wanted, and she said he wanted to see me again. We had one brief meeting in college, but he stayed in to study that night, and then I never heard from him again. He swears that he called me and spoke to one of my roommates and that they just didn't give me the message. I believe him, but we've joked about it ever since. During this gap in time that we were not connected, Derek was also living in Florida. Later, when I found this out, I found it interesting how parallel our experiences were at the time. I had no idea that he was so close to me.

I asked Molly if he knew I had a baby, and she said, "Yes, and his parents also know." She shared that on a joint family vacation with her boyfriend and his family, she updated everyone on my new life circumstances and that I was taking on motherhood as a single mom.

I thought, "Wow, okay…" It was kind of an exciting thought that I might be accepted by not only a guy I had an interest in, but possibly his family, too. However, I worried about my body, how I looked, and all I had been through. I feared the judgment of others. I knew for myself that I had done the right thing, but I didn't feel worthy of someone who had their whole life ahead of them without attachments or responsibilities. There was no time for me or dating. I was working and raising a child. However, I agreed to meet him and see him again.

Being the man of action that he is, he drove up that same weekend from Southern Oregon and popped into my work. I remember exactly what he was wearing and the silver briefcase he was carrying. I was thinking, "Wow, impressive. He just graduated college and is already carrying a briefcase." He was serious about his future, and I was immediately attracted to his professional appearance and drive, even if he was just trying to impress me!

I was very nervous, but surprisingly at ease with him. We visited in the community room at the complex where I worked and talked easily together. During this time, we made plans to meet up that weekend at Molly's. Once I was with him for a few minutes in person, I didn't feel as nervous, and a little excitement set in for the time with some friends and the possibilities that could be.

Later that evening, I was at Molly's house when Derek walked in. I scurried into the kitchen because, again, the nerves set in. I just really lacked confidence in myself. I was terrified of what others' opinions were. My body was not what it was before. I had to ask my parents to watch Paige, who was still very young, to go out and socialize for a few hours. A lot was happening very fast, and I hadn't had a lot of time to focus on my healing or process why I had landed in this place in my life.

How Bullying Experiences Change Your Life

In high school, I received an award at the senior breakfast for the "best body." I didn't get the best personality, smartest, best smile, or most likely to succeed; I got the "best body." There were some definite implications for receiving this award, both internally and relationally. When I stood out for anything, it seemed like I was cut out of girls' groups. This happened repeatedly in middle school and high school. Sometimes, it was because a boy liked me that another girl liked, and so there was jealousy. At times, girls would be mean, and I wouldn't know why. For me, I internalized extreme pressure, which started even before this award was given, to be perfect, to eat the right things, and not get fat, and it put an extreme focus on my body. I thought I had to be perfect to be successful in life and relationships, and I did not feel safe or confident in connecting with people.

This started in high school when I dated a guy who was obsessed with his appearance and thin, beautiful women. He would jokingly suggest that I eat cucumbers to stay thin. I'll never forget that conversation with him. I believed I would not be lovable if I had an ounce of fat on me. I later found out his dad cheated on his mom, and so he followed suit. He cheated on me in high school when I backed out of the senior trip to Mexico. Unsurprisingly, the girl was a beautiful swimsuit model who was in magazines that I could find at the store. I remember feeling a profound sense of betrayal from many of my friends who were there, knowing he was spending time with another girl. No one shared it with me.

When he finally told me, I was devastated, and I felt like such a sucker. I developed an extreme complex about how I looked and really struggled to let go of this person. There were other unhealthy things happening in this relationship, but I was struggling to feel confident in myself. My self-worth became attached to his opinion of me and whether he wanted me or not. He would make fun of my faith, my family, and other things. Looking back, it's interesting to see that what he was making fun of is now one of the most highly valued things in my life. One example is when my dad would call family meetings so we could stay close and communicate, share our values, and plan our calendars.

It's so funny that these are all things that are important to me today, my strengths, and things I help people with as a coach, but in my desire to please him and keep him, I let them slip. I let him erode my sense of self until there was almost nothing recognizable left. The keywords here are "I let him!"

These experiences not only damaged my self-confidence, but also created a feeling of needing to defend myself in all my relationships. When I met my husband, this pattern resurfaced. I learned I needed to heal from jumping to the worst-case scenario in communications in relationships and trying to defend myself. I eventually learned to trust people again.

Personal Examples of Bullying

In school, I had many experiences with bullying, and I later found that bullying in school, when left unhealed, can have profound and lasting effects that can change the course of one's life. I didn't understand any of this until more recently, which is why I am sharing it with you in this book. I had a vague awareness of the impact, but I also carried the lion's share of the blame, shame, and judgment that came with that. I noticed I was triggered regularly and often by relationships, especially by people who were insensitive or controlling. I would have knee-jerk reactions to fight and tell them off. It still happens from time to time. I get triggered by comments that feel belittling, insulting, or controlling and take it very personally. It happens a lot less now than it did in the past after I did some work on it and became much more aware of where it comes from.

The emotional scars and trauma from being bullied can linger well into adulthood, impacting self-esteem, relationships, and mental health. Unresolved trauma may lead to feelings of insecurity, anxiety, and even depression, inhibiting personal growth and success. Survivors of bullying might also develop coping mechanisms or defense mechanisms that, while initially helpful, can become obstacles to forming healthy connections and engaging in life fully. The lasting impact of unhealed bullying underscores the importance of addressing and processing these experiences through therapy, support networks, and self-care, as it can pave the way for healing, resilience, and a brighter future.

Throughout my journey from elementary to high school, I encountered a series of challenging experiences with bullying that have profoundly shaped my perspective and resilience. These stories of adversity, triumph, and personal growth are a testament to the power of resilience, inner strength, and the unwavering belief in oneself. As I share my encounters with bullying, my hope is not only to shed light on the lasting impact it can have but also to inspire others who may be navigating similar struggles, showing that it's possible to emerge from such trials with greater resilience and self-confidence.

Elementary School

In 1986, Diana moved to our school. She was wealthy and fashionable. She lived in a desirable neighborhood with large, beautiful homes in it. She wore all Guess clothing; I wanted all her outfits! I basically idolized her, as did the other girls, as she was pretty, funny, and a leader. Later, I came to understand it wasn't healthy leadership; it was superficial and controlling, but back then, when you're young and enamored with the cool factor, it's easy to get sucked in.

She had an older sister and was going through puberty sooner than most of the rest of us. She would show us signs of it, too. I was quite innocent and only had a younger brother, so she was advancing much quicker. I remember one time she had us comparing how much pubic hair we had at a sleepover by showing it to each other. I don't know if any of you did this crazy stuff, but we did it at her direction. We laughed a lot when hanging out together and I got to do things my parents would never let us do, including watching *Nightmare on Elm Street* at a fourth-grade sleepover birthday party. I clearly was not ready for it and had nightmares for months after that. I developed a fear of falling asleep because I thought Freddy Krueger was real and would get me while I slept. I became afraid to take a shower because I thought he would come out of the drain.

Diana had so much control over the group of girls I was running with at one point. When she would leave for the Talented and Gifted program (TAG) on Fridays and come back later that day, she would have girls confessing who "took over." This could be anything from suggesting we go to the swing set or encouraging someone to play wall ball or kiss a boy on the playground. She would investigate and find out who was too confident that day for her liking and then unleash the group on them. This usually looked like shunning you, excluding your participation in the playground activities or playdates after school, and purposely leaving you out.

My time finally came when I was uninvited to the coolest Halloween party coming up. She was throwing a Halloween party in the clubhouse with boys and girls invited. I had been invited and was looking forward to this party. It was the event of the year for the sixth-grade popular kids, and I was included. After she found out that I suggested everyone go to the swings (I loved the swings), she had someone else tell me I was no longer invited to the party.

Like the betrayal of all my friends in high school when my boyfriend cheated on me, all the girls went along with it, and I became chopped liver. No one would talk to me, and I cried for days. My mom felt so bad for me, but what was she to do? Suddenly, all my friends turned on me, and I had to sit at home on Halloween that year, wondering how much fun everyone was having without me.

Telling this story makes me want to give my inner child a big hug; it brings tears to my eyes, and it breaks my heart to think of anyone going through something similar. This experience changed me, but it wasn't the last, unfortunately.

Middle School

In 1988, I had moved up to middle school. Many of my friends were wealthy and lived in amazing homes. We had a lot of sleepovers at girlfriends' houses. I experienced my own version of awe and sometimes envy being friends with them. I remember wanting to borrow their clothes or thinking how nice it must be to live in such a cool, beautiful house.

I was trying out modeling in middle school and had taken a modeling course at John Casablanca. I remember being so nervous about doing it, but I wanted to learn how to be poised and put together. I loved fashion, so I signed up for the ramp modeling course, where we learned everything about modeling. I had to leave a sleepover early and remember walking out; I can still visualize the hallway in the beautiful home we were in, and I said "goodbye" to the group of girls, the mom hosting, and her friend, another mom.

I remember feeling uncomfortable around this one mom; she was very negative and nitpicky. Later that week, one of the friends who was there at that moment came to me and told me that as I was leaving, this mom said, "Where is she going?"

One of the girls replied, "Oh, she's going to a ramp modeling thing."

The mom responded with, "Do you mean 'tramp' modeling?"

Apparently, this elicited some laughter and made the one friend who shared it with me uncomfortable, which is why she shared it. I was devastated and internalized the criticism. I remember being so shocked that a mother would say something like this in a group setting; I didn't know what to do.

However, I did find it easier to get along with boys. They were just funny and seemed to have a lot less drama. I even dated a couple that we held hands at school or met up at friends' houses. When I had my first kiss in seventh grade, the other girls decided they didn't like me and sent me nasty anonymous letters that hurt me to my core. I developed severe anxiety about being liked and going to school. Slowly, I was developing a mixture of very high sensitivity to criticism and a very low tolerance as well; anger was brewing, and the sadness was overwhelming at times. I just kept going and tried to be strong and hide it.

High School

The year I entered high school was 1990. It was a fresh start. I worked hard on friendships and had a boyfriend. I developed people-pleasing behavior and had an awareness of the trauma that happened to my mom when I was a young girl, but I did not know how to process it, so it just lingered with me like a dark cloud. During my first year in high school, I began receiving death threats over the phone at my house. I was scared to go to school, but I didn't want anyone to know. My parents insisted on calling the police and had the calls traced to a girl's house that went to my school. I had never had a problem with her and barely knew her. She was a year older. I learned through this experience that even acquaintances aren't safe.

I found it safer to be with my guy friends over the girls. My experiences with many girls had felt unreliable. I liked that hanging around with the guys was less dramatic and just felt easier. But, on yet another occasion, I was out at the river with a couple of guy friends, and two older girls, twin sisters, were out there the same day. Suddenly, the girls approached me on the beach and said that they had been instructed to throw me in the water. This was my first physical threat of bullying. Shocked, I began to feel like I was going to cry. I don't even remember what I said, and luckily, the guys that were with me had my back and didn't allow it. They quickly scooped me up, and we went to the car and left. I cried all the way home. It was humiliating to be pointed out and targeted in a public setting and, on top of it, to show emotion. I felt weak and embarrassed for crying and needing their help to leave what was otherwise shaping up to be a fun day of hanging out.

Within the same year, I lost a girlfriend to suicide. She overdosed on pills. As I desperately tried to understand how someone so bright could want to take her own life, I learned she was in an abusive, controlling relationship with her boyfriend, an older student from our school. She was struggling with depression and self-confidence. It hit me hard because, when I heard a bit of her story, I resonated with it and felt her pain. And even more difficult, I didn't know she felt this way. I couldn't have helped her because I didn't know. She was always bubbly and fun and sweet. Her memorial service was one of the saddest things I have ever experienced in my life. In my desperate need of reassurance during this tragic time, I remembered sitting in the church, grasping for something that was written on the funeral program. It was the Bible verse about seasons.

[1] For everything there is a season, a time for every activity under heaven. [2] A time to be born and a time to die. A time to plant and a time to harvest (Ecclesiastes 3:1–2).

It all just felt so senseless and sad and deepened the sadness I already felt.

WHAT I'VE LEARNED

Looking back on it now, I see that the guy I dated in high school who cheated on me was very insecure and very focused on physicality. In his mind, I don't think it was a priority for him to date women with great personalities. I had been influenced to place value into something transient and changing; I had allowed him to push me to focus on things that were maybe on the top of his value list but entirely superficial, and none of it meshed with how I grew up or believed. Now, as a mom of three girls, I encourage our girls to set the boundaries for the relationships they are in, I see that this may not have been a personality flaw in him; it just might have been a result of his age, hormones, and maturity.

I had a lot of friends in high school and several boyfriends in those years. I always tried to be kind to people because I knew how it felt to be on the receiving end of unkindness and cruelty. I did have some changing friend groups, however, and ended up being left out. Looking back, however, I see that this was a blessing, and mostly about our common interests changing. We were all growing, self-centered, and trying to grow up.

The external implications of winning the "best body" award in high school (which, the more I look at it, I can't believe was even allowed) were that it further increased the divide between me and other girls in my class. I guess it was the 90s, and things were different then! High school girls learn to fit in, not to stick out ... at least I tried. To this day, I compare, too, so I must constantly check myself for comparing myself to others. It is a human tendency that takes work to overcome.

As I went through my bullying experiences in my youth, I internalized the labels and criticism. When we are young, we often internalize the hurtful labels and negative messages that result from bullying. These labels can leave deep emotional scars and influence self-perception, self-worth, and overall confidence. However, it's important to remember that we are incredibly resilient and can overcome these challenges with the right support and guidance. By providing a safe and nurturing environment, instilling a sense of self-worth, and fostering open communication, parents, caregivers, and educators can help reframe those negative labels and develop a positive self-image. Encouraging activities that promote self-discovery and self-expression, like sports, arts, or hobbies, can also aid in rebuilding self-esteem. I do think schools have done a better job in recent years placing importance on empathy, kindness, and respect for others and creating a culture of inclusivity, reducing the chances of bullying and the lasting impact of negative labels. This kind of support can help individuals to rewrite their self-narrative, emerging from the shadow of bullying with renewed strength and self-assurance.

Whatever worked in the past, build on it; whatever didn't work in the past, break the chain that binds you to it.

Marianne Williamson

The awareness around all these experiences has shaped me into the person I am today; I realize that now. It has also created a whole new perspective on how I have learned to love myself and approach relationships.

I am grateful I had God because I now know that this is what kept me going when things were stacking up, and I was developing a very succinct radar for people in pain and a strong desire to alleviate it in any way I could. I hope that you are beginning to believe that you can also heal. Keep going.

WHAT YOU CAN DO

Unpack why you hide. What does it look like to unpack your trauma when so much of it has stacked up? It looks like taking the time to look at your stuff, and by your stuff, I don't mean yours; I mean the accumulation of lies that have attached themselves to you.

Humans believe so many lies because we aren't aware. We ignore the truth, or we just don't see the truth. When we are educated, we accumulate a lot of knowledge, and all that knowledge is just like a wall of fog that doesn't allow us to perceive the truth, what really is.

Don Miguel Ruiz

It's difficult to see the truth when you are under a pile of debris. I like to use the metaphor of a remodel when thinking about big changes in my emotional life. Imagine for a moment you've found your dream property. It sits on a hill and has a beautiful view of the ocean, but it has a run-down house on it. Its structure is tilted, the roof is caving in, and even the foundation is crumbling in some areas and hanging over the edge of a hillside. You just have a feeling this is where you are supposed to live. Something about it feels like home, but it has so many issues, and you know it will be a lot of work to get it cleaned up. You are constantly chasing the leaks and the broken parts to keep the house livable. This is what it's like when you've been through trauma, abuse, bullying, and lots of hurt. You feel broken, afraid, tired, and alone; parts of you are almost unrecognizable, and you aren't sure who to talk to.

Some of the first steps you can take when entering a remodel include checking the foundation and collecting the right team of knowledgeable experts to help you assess the damage and current state of the property. You would never begin replacing light fixtures first thing in a run-down house. Sadly, this is what many of us do. We get some plastic surgery; we go shopping; we find another guy to date; we move to a new town. We do all the surface things to fix the problem, suck it up and move on. This could appear to work for a while until the patch you did on the wall begins to leak because the broken pipe in the wall was never repaired and continues to leak and seep through the wall. The "ick" stays in you until you choose to look at it and unpack it.

I'm hoping that if you are going through something right now, that doesn't feel right or you've allowed trauma from your past to accumulate, you will at least allow yourself to sit in the discomfort, even for just a minute. Sometimes, when we have been through something hard, it's easy just to push forward and try to cover up what we are ashamed of and the painful moments for fear of looking and feeling weak.

I just saw a meme of a cartoon character carrying a heavy load of boxes that said, "Remember, if you're not speaking it, you're storing it, and that sh*t gets heavy!" I'll add to that, "If you're not unpacking it, you're storing it, and that sh*t gets super heavy!" For those of you who have had challenges with bullying and toxic relationships, I pray this helps you also unpack your stories.

When you begin to journal about it, go to therapy to discuss it, find a trusted friend to really unpack the stories one by one, or better yet, ask for support, you begin to understand how they make you feel. Take the time to answer the reflection questions while unpacking your story.

REFLECTION QUESTIONS

Really think about how the abuse and bullying have changed your life and the decisions you've made because of the coping and defense mechanisms you learned from being mistreated. Use the reflection questions below to help you get started.[10]

1. What happened?
2. Why did you choose this relationship?
3. What attracted you to them and why?
4. What did you learn from being in this relationship?
5. What kind of relationship do you have with yourself? Do you criticize yourself over every little mistake, or do you talk to yourself supportively?
6. Which relationship is the most important for you now, the one you cherish the most?
7. Which relationships make you feel empty or distressed?

---

10   Chantal McCullighOwner at Anxiety GoneChantal McCulligh is a mental health entrepreneur, "Self-Therapy Questions to Ask Yourself to Start Your Healing -," Anxiety Relief and Mental Health, October 31, 2023, https://anxiety-gone.com/self-therapy-questions-to-ask-yourself-to-start-your-healing/.

8. Are you happy in your personal life with your partner or spouse? Do you have a healthy relationship?

9. Which relationships guilt-trip you or make you question your self-worth, self-confidence, and decision-making abilities?

10. Who is the person in your life with whom you need to spend more time or less time?

11. Which relationship do you despise but must put up with for several reasons?

12. Do people close to you make you feel better or worse about yourself?

13. What bothers you about the people close to you?

14. Do you judge people often?

15. Do you get angry and defensive when someone disagrees with you? Why?

16. Are you ready to start a family? If you already have children, are you doing enough for them?

ACTION STEP: TRAUMA HEALING JOURNALING

Before you begin journaling, find a notebook and a favorite pen. You can keep more than one notebook, too. One you can use for journaling for trauma healing and one for gratitude expression and other random thoughts and feelings. The idea is to start a journal with an intention. Your notebook is yours, but you can choose to share your journaling with people you trust.

Here are some tips to begin journaling for trauma healing:

• Sit in a quiet place and find a time when fewer distractions surround you. You can choose to write in your journal during your bus commute, during your lunch break at work, or in the evening before bed.

- Always try to take a few minutes before you begin journaling. Let yourself think about how your trauma has affected your life.
- Once you're done writing for the day, pay close attention to how you're feeling. Notice any change in your emotions and thoughts after your journaling.
- Don't worry too much about grammar and spelling. Keep your focus on transferring your thoughts and feelings into the journal.
- Be as descriptive as you can. When you're writing about your feelings, also write about the thoughts these feelings bring forth. How do your actions connect with these feelings? This can help increase your body-mind awareness and bring attention to your emotions and thoughts.
- Keep track of your feelings so you can come back and look at how your emotions, feelings, and thoughts have changed since you began journaling.
- Be kind to your thoughts. Let your words flow without any judgment. However, avoid rushing through your journaling. Think about the prompts you're using carefully before writing about your experiences.

CHAPTER 4

RELATIONSHIP HEALTH: ATTACHMENT AND ABUSE

We do learn so much about ourselves in our experiences. But also, know that it shouldn't have happened. This was not a lesson you needed to learn.
Jordan Pickell, trauma therapist

When Derek arrived that day at Molly's house, I was stunned at how he treated me. He probably noticed I was shy and avoiding him. He didn't let that stop him. He followed me right into the kitchen and struck up a conversation. I felt immediately comfortable with him. He didn't look me up and down or show the slightest judgment or concern about my body shape or size. He looked at me like I was the most beautiful woman in the world. I'm not sure if that's what he was thinking; he tells me he was very attracted to me, but I felt something very loving and accepting. It was a natural feeling; I felt relaxed right away. I still felt very vulnerable and raw from my experiences and learning how to be a mom, but there was a different connection happening, which was very clear.

He wasn't focused on my body. I remember later he told me it was my face he loved. He thought I was beautiful. This was such a change from previous situations that it was refreshing. For me, when I became a mom, everything changed. I wanted to be good for my daughter; I wanted to be an example for her; I wanted to be a better person. Derek and I had a short courtship and an extraordinary romance. He held my hand on the way to the bars in Portland that night. We sat across from each other, didn't even drink, and talked the whole night until we had to help our friends get home.

He told me within two weeks that he wanted to be Paige's dad and proposed marriage with a silver ring he wore in college when we were there for a football game. No one knew he did that. It was our little secret. My parents cautiously watched what was happening after my daughter was born. From a parent's perspective, I'm sure it was scary for them to see me dating so soon. The saving grace was that it was Molly who introduced us, and they (and I) had always loved Molly and knew she was a person with solid values who likely wouldn't introduce me to an unworthy suitor.

Derek would drive up every weekend from Southern Oregon to Portland to see Paige and me. One night, while watching TV, a commercial for our childhood hit movie, *ET,* came on the screen. Derek and I both raised our fingers toward the television and said, "ET," in the infamous ET character voice, just like ET in the movie. That was the day we named our brains to be of the same series, C-22. They say when you can complete each other's sentences, you've found your soul mate. I was starting to believe I had found mine. Someone as weird as that doesn't come along every day, and I've always considered myself a little weird!

After a month or more of dating, Derek brought me a card and a gift. The gift was a CD of Space Ghost, a very strange classic animated character, a bizarre creation that captures the essence of surreal humor. How romantic, right? Receiving this amazing first gift from Derek foreshadowed what I was in for: a weird and wonderful adventure in love and raising a family with a man who found great humor in nonsensical conversations.

Space Ghost is an intergalactic superhero who moonlights as a talk show host in "Space Ghost Coast to Coast." The show's eccentric humor and absurd scenarios were ahead of its time, paving the way for a new wave of animated absurdity. Derek said he loved me in that card, and I hastily put it away as I wasn't sure if I was ready to open my heart that quickly and accept the love.

It would be years of work to build back my confidence before I felt completely worthy of him. I do believe he was a gift from God. The sense of humor and silliness sprinkled with that bit of the weird that felt like home helped me navigate healing from the pile of debris that had accumulated in my heart. Find a sense of humor! It is a necessary ingredient to healing.

ATTACHMENT STYLES

As we grow, peers and romantic partners will often take over the role of the primary attachment figure. As I began to understand this, I realized that even with mostly healthy parents, I could slip into low self-worth from my interactions with others and develop a less secure attachment style. Persistent bullying, a cruel partner, or a devastating breakup could cause a person to develop an insecure attachment style in adult life. As I learned this, I realized I needed to work on my self-worth because of what I learned from friendships and dating early on.

I internalized labels and criticism from my experiences with bullying. Here are just a few that I accumulated. You may recognize some of these.

- Acquaintances aren't safe.
- Other adults are mean and cruel.
- My family values were silly or weird, including my faith.
- If I shined in any way, I would be left out, punished, and alone.
- I had to be thin and hot, according to someone else's definition, to be loved.
- If I didn't do what my boyfriends wanted me to do, I would be left alone.
- Friends don't have each others' back (when other friends betray them).

I won't say that all my experiences with people were negative. However, when you experience trauma and toxic relationships, it tends to weigh heavily on you, becoming the only thing you see. It reinforces behavior patterns like hiding yourself, not caring for yourself, pleasing others, giving up your values to fit in, and just a general lack of self-confidence.

It can be helpful to understand what our attachment style is and what a healthy relationship looks like. Securely attached people feel they are worthy of love, and they can build healthy, long-lasting relationships. This result comes from feeling safe, cared for, and loved during your first years of life. Your caregivers were likely in touch with their own emotions and aware of their emotions and behaviors. Children will imitate what their caregivers do, so if they are secure themselves and emotionally aware, it's likely that you learned this too. Look at the following list and circle the ones that you feel are true for you.

- Ability to regulate your emotions.
- Easily trusting others.
- Effective communication skills.
- Ability to seek emotional support.
- Comfortable being alone.

- Comfortable in close relationships.
- Ability to self-reflect in partnerships.
- Being easy to connect with.
- Ability to manage conflict well.
- High self-esteem.
- Ability to be emotionally available.

According to Psych Central, "People with secure attachment styles tend to navigate relationships well. They're generally positive, trusting, and loving to their partners."[11] It helped me see that most of the people I went to school with, especially the ones that I had a hard time with, were likely not raised by secure attachment-style parents.

Once I learned about the secure attachment style, I became a bit confused because, for the most part, I felt that my parents were. Upon further examination of the attachment styles, I realized that a mostly secure parent could raise you, but have something happen that changes this for them, or something like bullying happens to you and changes it for you. Unless you process this, it will change how you approach and attach in future relationships. Most of us don't even understand what's happening or that we need to process it, so we just carry it around with us for a lifetime, wondering why we continually have difficulty trusting in relationships and feeling valued and supported.

WHAT AN UNHEALTHY RELATIONSHIP LOOKS LIKE

In unhealthy relationships, one partner tries to control and exert power over the other physically, sexually, or emotionally. Abuse is a *pattern* of behavior, meaning that it happens more

---

11   Morgan Mandriota, "4 Types of Attachment: What's Your Style?," Psych Central, October 13, 2021, https://psychcentral.com/health/4-attachment-styles-in-relationships.

than once. However, when a romantic partner does any one of these acts—even once—it's still considered "*dating violence*." Sadly, unhealthy or abusive relationships are common.

Let's go back to my years in elementary school (see Elementary School section in Chapter 3). A so-called friend was controlling a group of girls by telling others what to do, telling them to exclude others or leave someone out. Statistics say that once it has happened the first time, it is much more likely to happen again. Mount Sinai Adolescent Health Center states: "An unhealthy relationship might involve a power imbalance, being mean, ignoring boundaries, or pressuring one person to do things they aren't comfortable with. In an abusive relationship, one partner has almost complete control of the other."[12]

In middle school, it became more direct, and the girls used intimidation and threatening letters. To exert control over me, they wanted to instill fear and watch me struggle so I would go away. They didn't like the competition for attention. Little did they know we didn't have to compete. There was plenty of space for all of us! In high school, it was again a girl I barely knew, thinking it would be fun to intimidate someone younger to mark her territory so I wouldn't take anything from her. The funny thing is, as far as I knew, we didn't like the same boys, and I wasn't even in her peer group. I was left to guess why she didn't like me. Maybe she felt threatened by me, or maybe she just felt powerful, scaring a younger person.

STATISTICS ON BULLYING

Until I started therapy later in life, in my thirties and forties, I had no idea what was hidden inside me, festering and

---

12   "Unhealthy or Abusive Relationships," Mount Sinai Adolescent Health Center, November 5, 2020, https://www.teenhealthcare.org/article/unhealthy-relationships/.

eroding my confidence. It was like storing a big pile of filth in my heart. This may be a gross metaphor, but maybe you can relate. One of the biggest steps to overcoming what you are going through is understanding what is and isn't okay and what is at work in your life. We may feel that something is wrong and we are hurting, but we don't really know that we are not alone. Bullying is much more common than I originally thought. While going through it, I felt like it was just me. If you've been bullied, you know how lonely it can feel. Here are some important statistics to understand.

- A national survey found that 1 in 3 teens reported being verbally or psychologically abused, and 1 in 10 had been the victims of physical dating violence within the past year.[13]
- One out of every five (20.2 percent) students report being bullied.
- Of those, 41 percent indicated that they think the bullying would happen again.
- Additionally, 13 percent were made fun of, called names, or insulted; another 13 percent were the subject of rumors; 5 percent were pushed, shoved, tripped, or spit on; and another 5 percent were excluded from activities on purpose.

After hearing these statistics, are you recalling experiences you've had or others around you? When I finally got help, I was shocked at what I learned from these toxic relationships and bullying.

---

13   "Student Reports of Bullying Results from the 2017 School Crime Supplement to the National Crime Victimization Survey," U.S. Department of Education, July 2019, https://nces.ed.gov/pubs2019/2019054.pdf.

Warning Signs of An Unhealthy Relationship

If you are in the middle of what feels like an unhealthy relationship, here are the types of abuse in toxic relationships so you can identify them. If you think you are in a toxic relationship, take note, even circle the ones that resonate with you or sound familiar. Doing the uncomfortable work of understanding what kind of relationship you are in can be an incredible, courageous act of self-love. Be patient with yourself; this will not create overnight change. You also don't need a reason to end an unhealthy relationship if you identify it as such.

Here are some of the warning signs I learned are signs of an unhealthy relationship. I discuss each of these further in this chapter.

- Emotional, Verbal, and Psychological Abuse
- Physical Abuse
- Sexual Abuse
- Reproductive Coercion
- Financial Abuse
- Stalking

Emotional, Verbal, and Psychological Abuse

Emotional, verbal, and psychological abuse is a pattern of behavior in which the perpetrator insults, humiliates, and generally instills fear in an individual to control them. The individual's reality may become distorted as they internalize the abuse as their own failings.[14]

---

14   "Emotional Abuse," Psychology Today, accessed September 27, 2023, https://www.psychologytoday.com/gb/basics/emotional-abuse.

- **Jealousy:** Your partner is extremely jealous. They get angry or resentful when you talk to someone else or hang out with someone besides them. They might demand access to your phone or social media accounts or frequently accuse you of flirting.
- **Anger:** Your partner picks fights with you, screams, or yells at you. You feel like you must change your behavior to avoid upsetting your partner.
- **Name-Calling:** Your partner calls you names, says you're worthless, makes fun of you, or puts you down in other ways.
- **Dishonesty:** Your partner lies to you, keeps information from you, or steals from you.
- **Dependence:** Your partner says that they can't live without you and threatens to do something drastic (like hurt or kill themselves) if you end the relationship.
- **Threats:** Your partner threatens to hurt you or a pet or destroy something you own. They may also threaten to spread a rumor, tell a secret, or share nude or sexual photos or videos. They may threaten to kill or hurt themselves if you leave them. You may feel afraid, or like they'll ruin your life if you don't do what they say. In LGBTQ+ relationships, this might mean threatening to "out" you to friends or family.
- **Isolation:** Your partner tries to keep you from seeing your friends or family. They might get angry or jealous when you spend time without them, guilt trip you into canceling plans, or try to convince you that your other relationships don't matter. You and your partner spend almost all your time together, and you feel guilty when you're apart.
- **Lack of Trust:** Your partner asks for your passwords, demands access to your social media or phone, or wants to know where you are and what you're always doing.

They accuse you of hiding something or lying to them. You may feel guilty for wanting any privacy.

- **Catfishing:** Your partner pretends to be someone else online and flirts with you to "catch" you cheating.
- **Denial:** They may "gaslight" you by denying their actions, saying you remember something wrong, or minimizing the importance of something they did or said. Or they may blame you for their actions.

Physical Abuse

Physical abuse is deliberately aggressive or violent behavior by one person toward another that results in bodily injury. It is most frequently observed in relationships of trust, particularly between parents and children or between intimate partners (e.g., in a marriage or other relationship).

Individuals who experience physical abuse often feel helpless and isolated and are prone to the subsequent development of numerous pathological conditions, including depression, eating disorders, PTSD, anxiety disorders, and substance use problems.[15]

- Hitting, slapping, shoving, or punching.
- Spitting.
- Pinching.
- Kicking.
- Choking or strangling.
- Throwing something at you.
- Pulling your hair.
- Causing any other kind of physical pain.

---

15 "Physical Abuse and Violence," American Psychological Association, accessed September 27, 2023, https://www.apa.org/topics/physical-abuse-violence.

Sexual Abuse

Sexual abuse is any sexual activity that occurs without consent. Also referred to as sexual assault or sexual violence, it includes unwanted sexual touching, forced oral sex, and rape, among other sexual acts. No matter which act occurs, it's not the survivor's fault that they were assaulted.[16]

- Any unwanted sexual touch, including kissing.
- Rape or sexual assault.
- Forcing, coercing, or pressuring you into having sex or doing something sexual against your will or without your consent.
- Pressuring you to have sex without condoms or other barrier methods.
- Pressuring you to have sex or do something sexual at a time or in a place you do not want to.
- Getting you drunk or drugging you before sex.

Reproductive Coercion

Reproductive coercion refers to behavior "that interferes with the autonomous decision-making of a woman, with regard to reproductive health." In a 2018 systematic review, Grace and Anderson identified three interconnected forms of reproductive coercion: birth control sabotage, pregnancy coercion (threatening or pressuring a partner to get pregnant), and abortion coercion (threatening or pressuring a partner to get or not get an abortion).[17]

---

16 "Sexual Abuse," Psychology Today, accessed September 27, 2023, https://www.psychologytoday.com/us/basics/sexual-abuse.

17 "Reproductive Coercion, Post-Roe," Psychology Today, accessed September 27, 2023, https://www.psychologytoday.com/us/blog/awareness-action/202206/reproductive-coercion-post-roe.

- Sabotaging or controlling your birth control, such as poking holes in condoms, flushing birth control pills down the toilet, or removing condoms during sex without your consent.
- Forcing or pressuring you to have or not have an abortion.
- Pressuring you into stopping birth control.
- Forcing you to have unprotected sex.

Financial Abuse

Financial abuse is a form of bullying to manipulate or control the other person, often to improve their own financial circumstance. Financial abuse and neglect are often invisible forms of domestic violence and can also occur in business partnerships and workplaces. Some financial abuse involves unlawful or criminal behaviors.[18]

- Preventing you from getting a job or sabotaging your work.
- Keeping you from going to work (for example, by taking your car keys).
- Guilt tripping or coercing you into quitting your job.
- Saying or doing something to make you get fired.
- Taking or stealing your paycheck or student loan check.
- Using your financial situation to control you (for example, if you are reliant on them for rent, food, or other necessities, they may threaten to stop supporting you).
- Controlling how you spend your own money.

---

18   "Are You a Victim of Financial Abuse or Neglect?," Psychology Today, accessed September 27, 2023, https://www.psychologytoday.com/us/blog/mental-wealth/202209/are-you-victim-financial-abuse-or-neglect.

Stalking

Stalking is a pattern of unwanted contact or behavior that leads someone to feel upset, anxious, or scared for their safety. Stalking is a consistent and intentional pattern of behavior, as opposed to one or two isolated incidents. It persists after the individual has asked the stalker to stop contacting them.[19]

- Memorizing your schedule or following you and showing up where you are or they think you might be.
- Sending unwanted or excessive flowers, letters, or other gifts.
- Tracking what you do online or who you call or text.
- Extensively researching you on the internet.
- Damaging or threatening your property or people you know.
- Other behavior that makes you feel afraid or monitored.

These are all abusive behaviors. They are NEVER normal, and no one EVER deserves them. You deserve a relationship based on kindness and respect.

WHAT A HEALTHY RELATIONSHIP LOOKS LIKE

A healthy relationship will never require you to sacrifice your friends, your dreams, or your dignity.
Dinkar Kalotra

I think you get the point. So now what? I think it's important to understand what a healthy relationship looks like.

---

19 "Stalking," Psychology Today, accessed September 27, 2023, https://www.psychologytoday.com/us/basics/stalking.

I remember my parents teaching me that in a healthy marriage or relationship, the physical side is fleeting. Hopefully, when you find the right person, you will have intimacy and affection and be attracted to the person, but the reality is our bodies change over time, and the human side of things changes all the time. If there is too much focus on the outward appearance of things, sex, or having a great body, what happens when life happens, you have children, and that changes, etc.?

If I were to define a "healthy relationship," it would include a few key things. A healthy relationship is a relationship where both partners feel valued, respected, and supported. It is a relationship where both people can communicate openly and honestly and where they feel safe and comfortable with each other. Some key characteristics of a healthy relationship include:

- **Mutual Respect:** Both partners have respect for each other's feelings, opinions, and boundaries.
- **Effective Communication:** Both partners can communicate effectively with each other, and they listen to each other's opinions and concerns without judgment.
- **Trust and Honesty:** Both partners are honest and trustworthy with each other, and they feel comfortable sharing their thoughts and feelings.
- **Shared Values and Interests:** Both partners share common values and interests, and they support each other's passions and goals.
- **Equality:** Both partners have an equal say in the relationship, and decisions are made together.
- **Support:** Both partners support each other emotionally, physically, and mentally.
- **Independence:** Both partners can maintain their individuality and pursue their own interests while still being committed to the relationship.

- **Healthy Conflict Resolution:** Both partners can resolve conflicts in a healthy and respectful way, and they are willing to compromise and find solutions together.
- **Emotional Stability:** Both partners are emotionally stable and able to manage their own emotions without relying on the other person.

Overall, a healthy relationship is one where both partners feel valued, respected, and supported, and where they can communicate effectively and work together to overcome challenges.

BEING OKAY WITH BEING ALONE

There was a space between when I left Sam and when Derek came along. And in this space, a lot of healing took place. My body was changing, and my heart was beginning to break open. I was entering an entirely new phase of my life, looking at what kind of mom I wanted to become and trying to develop a full understanding of how I got here and what kind of relationship I had with God and myself. I reached out to God to show me the way.

I spent time on my own, focused on creating the life I wanted to live. When we are alone, we can focus entirely on our well-being and do the work. I highly recommend not skipping this part and filling the space. In the past, I would have filled up my time with distractions in the form of socializing or dating. Being pregnant changed how I thought about dating, and I started spending time doing things I was interested in again. I had always had a desire to help with homelessness, so I signed up to work at a homeless shelter in downtown Portland. I even slept there one night on the cold, uncomfortable gym floor.

I remember issuing diapers to families with babies and feeding them breakfast in the morning. Suddenly, I felt like my situation was not so difficult. I was supporting myself to live; my apartment was paid for through work, and I lived where I worked, so it would be convenient as a mom, and I had a good, solid job. I was feeling more positive and self-reliant. The confidence was coming back because I began building the foundation of my life, starting with my own mental and physical health and well-being.

Embarking on a healing journey can be a daunting task, especially when we are used to seeking comfort and companionship from others. However, there is immense value in spending time alone during this process.

What I've Learned

If we've been fortunate enough to have had a secure attachment in the past, or if we've never had it, we go out into the world and either are blessed with healthy relationships or repeat the same insecure attachment relationships. Toxic relationships caused me to unlearn what a loving relationship looks like.

Scar tissue is stronger than regular tissue.
Realize the strength.

Henry Rollins, American musician

In all the years of work with therapists, one of the standout teachings I received was to add to my relationship criteria: reciprocal relationships. She explained this to mean that there should be an equal give and take in a healthy relationship. As soon as I understood this concept, it was a game-changer for me. That teaching played in my head in many situations where I was tempted to devalue myself, and I began to ask for reciprocation or equal effort in friendships and relationships. I began to value my energy and let go of friends with whom I felt I was forcing the connection, where the energetic input was lopsided, and I was doing most of the work.

I used to think the worst thing in life was to end up all alone, but it's not. The worst thing in life is to end up with people that make you feel all alone.

Robin Williams

I just let them go, and I practiced doing it with love for myself and the other person. This was a very key point in my journey to freedom.

Solitude provides us with a unique opportunity to connect with ourselves, our thoughts, and our emotions. It allows us to be introspective and reflect on our experiences, which can be difficult to do when the opinions and judgments of others constantly surround us. When we spend time alone, we can tap into our inner wisdom and gain a deeper understanding of our needs, desires, and fears. This self-awareness is crucial for our healing journey as it helps us to identify areas in our lives that need attention and provides us with the tools to work through them.

Moreover, being alone can also help us to cultivate a sense of self-reliance and independence. When we rely on others to provide us with comfort and support, we run the risk of becoming overly dependent on them. This can create an unhealthy dynamic where we feel unable to take care of ourselves without the help of others. However, when we spend time alone, we are forced to confront our own limitations and develop the skills and resources we need to take care of ourselves. This self-sufficiency can be empowering and help us build resilience and confidence we can draw on throughout our healing journey and beyond.

What You Can Do

Now that you have some awareness of your relationships, what healthy ones look like, and what unhealthy ones also look like, you have the information to proceed with your rebuild. Maybe you've discovered that a remodel won't cut it, and you need to level your emotional home and start fresh. Whatever the level of your project is, you ARE WORTH the work. Learning to love yourself, all of you, is the best, most important work you will do in your lifetime. It is the least selfish thing you can do; a whole and happy person has the potential to create infinite ripples of blessings and positive changes in the world, ultimately creating a happier world! Is there anything better to focus your energy and time on than improving the lives of others?

BUT FIRST… focus on you and look inside the walls of your heart and mind. Clear out the lies, termites, mold, and dry rot to rebuild a strong foundation in the framework; you will then give others the idea to do the same. Pretty soon, there will be way more dream houses and lives than old junkers!

Take a moment to envision your dream life, aka your emotional home. Imagine if you healed the crud, were successful at the rebuild, and ended up with the dream at the end of it. What does that look like for you? How do you feel? What kind of relationships do you have? What successes are you celebrating and adding to your resumé or bucket list?

Just like putting the light fixtures up before checking the foundation and repairing the structure of a remodel project, we must go inside the walls of our own mind and understand what's going on in there. What kind of lies have we accepted from the abusive words that have been said to us repeatedly? How are we playing small to avoid criticism or being beaten up? Where did these ideas come from? This was a lesson you didn't need to learn! You will get through it, however, and the strength you garner from it will help you rebuild your emotional home.

REFLECTION QUESTIONS

Now it's time to write out in our journals what lies we have accepted from the world and the people we have known. It's also important to look at what kind of relationship you would like to have. Remember, you never attempt to build or remodel a home without a plan and a design to follow; the same goes for curating our relationship life. You are creating your dream life, and included in that is building healthy, supportive relationships both with yourself and with others. So, let's dig into that here.

1. What does a reciprocal relationship look like to you?
2. What does unconditional self-love mean to you?
3. Do you think there is such a thing as too much self-love?
4. Why do you think self-love is important?
5. How do you think your life would change if you started practicing self-love?
6. What's standing in the way of you accepting yourself?
7. Are you comfortable being alone? Why or why not?
8. What can you do to fill your own cup before helping others?
9. Where do you need to slow down in your life?
10. What are some self-love affirmations you could say to yourself?
    - I accept love from myself.
    - I can do anything I set my mind to.
    - I deserve love.
    - I embrace who I am.
    - I deserve good things.

ACTION STEP: ENVISION YOUR DREAM

- What's next? The remodel! It's time to clean out the termites, water leaks, and structural damage, and begin to rebuild. Before we can rebuild, we must have a plan and a clear picture of what a healthy relationship, your strong home, is made of. Of course, you want your home to be beautiful, but it must have a strong foundation first. So, begin with the foundation. Take a few moments to envision your dream life and relationships. Write a few thoughts about how that can look for you, and write your goals on paper so you can easily envision your dream life. THINK BIG. Draw a picture if that's helpful, find some images in magazines or on the computer as to what this vision looks like. (See mine below.)

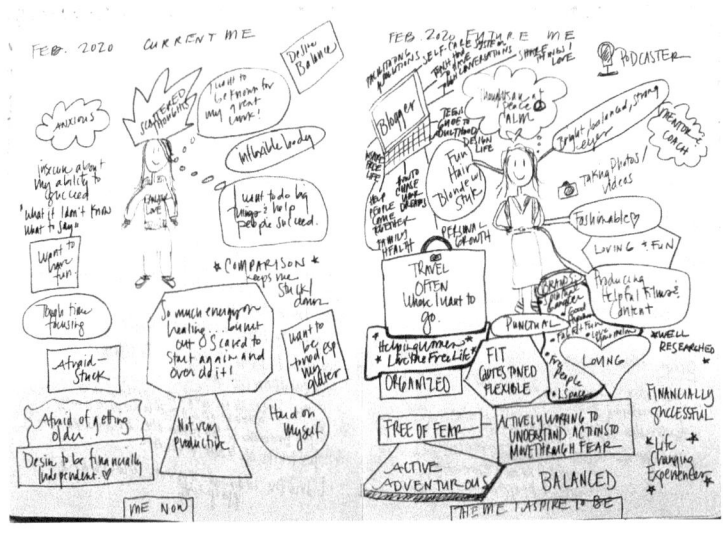

Current Me vs. Future Me - Create Your Dreamlife with Lavendaire[20]

---

20   Current Me vs. Future Me - Create Your Dreamlife with Lavendaire, https:// learn.lavendaire.com/courses

CHAPTER 5

SELF-EXPLORATION AND THE SPIRITUAL CONNECTION

When I discover who I am, I'll be free.
Ralph Ellison, Invisible Man

Picture a world where kindness reigns supreme, and the art of people-pleasing becomes a captivating dance with unforeseen consequences. As the storyteller, I'm going to share a fairytale and invite you to step into the magical realm where I, the unwitting protagonist, sought to find my joy through incessant people-pleasing. Little did I know that behind the veil of smiles and selfless acts lay a tale of self-discovery and the perils of neglecting one's own needs. Join me as I share this story, a profound journey from seeking approval to embracing authenticity. In sharing this narrative, I hope to illuminate the pitfalls of a life shaped solely by the desires of others and to inspire a deeper understanding of the delicate balance between kindness to the world and kindness to oneself. Characters have been fictionalized and combined into one countess, as this story repeated itself in many ways throughout my life.

Once upon a time, in the enchanting town of Harmonyville, there lived a young woman named Brooke DeBoer. Brooke was known far and wide for her unparalleled talent for people-pleasing. She possessed an innate ability to make everyone around her happy, and her kindness became legendary.

One day, Brooke received an invitation to organize the grand castle of Countess Diana, one of the most influential figures in Harmonyville. The countess, renowned for her lavish soirées, was preparing for the annual Moonlight Gala—a celebration attended by the town's elite.

Thrilled by the invitation, Brooke saw this as an opportunity to showcase her exceptional people-pleasing skills. She spent weeks meticulously planning every detail of the gala (keynote video, party, family Christmas, etc.), ensuring that each guest's desires were met. From the extravagant decorations to the personalized party favors, Brooke spared no effort in creating an event to remember.

As the Moonlight Gala approached, Brooke found herself tirelessly catering to the whims of the townspeople. Her eagerness to please became her sole focus, and she neglected her own needs and desires. The townspeople, enchanted by Brooke's dedication, showered her with praise and admiration.

The night of the Moonlight Gala arrived, and the castle glittered with an ethereal glow. The townspeople marveled at the grandeur Brooke had orchestrated. Yet, as the night unfolded, something unexpected happened. Countess Diana, usually poised and regal, began to feel overshadowed by Brooke's popularity.

Jealousy consumed the countess as she witnessed the guests gravitating towards Brooke. In a fit of rage, Countess Diana devised a plan to embarrass Brooke and reclaim the spotlight. She orchestrated a series of mishaps that turned the once-majestic gala into chaos.

Brooke, still oblivious to the countess's envy, tried desperately to salvage the evening. But the townspeople, now caught in the chaos, began to see through the façade. They realized Brooke's people-pleasing had blinded her to the manipulations around her.

In the end, the Moonlight Gala became a tale of caution in Harmonyville—a cautionary story of how excessive people-pleasing could backfire. Through a little self-exploration, Brooke learned that true happiness came from being authentic and standing up for herself, even if it meant disappointing others.

As the townspeople reflected on that fateful night, they remembered Brooke not for the extravagant gala (keynote video, documentary, party, etc.) but for the valuable lesson she unwittingly taught them: that the path to true harmony lies in balancing kindness to others with kindness to oneself.

And so, Brooke DeBoer's story became a cautionary chapter in the enchanted town's history, a reminder that even the most well-intentioned actions can have unforeseen consequences.

WHAT IS SELF-EXPLORATION?

Self-exploration is the practice of "taking a look at your own thoughts, feelings, behaviors, and motivations and asking why. It's looking for the roots of who we are—answers to all the questions we have about [ourselves]."[21] The hardest part for me in learning about myself was because it included everything: the good, bad, and ugly.

It's tough to work through the shame of the past, examining the decisions we've made to learn from them. It

---

21   Ryan Howes, Ph.D. (online, 2022) quoted in Michael Hovde, "Self-Exploration: Benefits and Tips for Getting Started," Psych Central, September 28, 2022, https://psychcentral.com/blog/self-exploration-getting-to-know-thyself.

would be much easier to blame others for our discomforts, judgments, and anything that's not going right in our lives. It would also have been easier to find something superficial to focus on, or at least, I thought. I did that, and it didn't really work. I had found this affirmation somewhere, and it sat on my desk as a reminder.

Internal power has less to do with money and worldly position and more to do with emotional expansiveness, spirituality, and conscious living.
Marianne Williamson

The same things kept repeating. I would work hard at everything and overtime to try to please people. Then the resentment would build, and I would feel so pissed off at the imbalance in my relationships. I would feel like I didn't have a voice, or I had to be a certain way to keep the relationship. I wouldn't honor my feelings or things I needed. Then I would be triggered and react; things would build up. I would lash out and feel like I needed to tell people off or put them in their place if they were being too controlling or opinionated about my life. My strength was emerging, but in all the wrong ways.

My husband and I were seeing a marriage counselor to work through some communication issues and to help us find ways to communicate through our differences—both from our upbringing and how we parented and approached life. The expectations of others weighed on us heavily, and we often would wear ourselves out, pleasing everyone else and not having much left for ourselves. The people-pleasing was coming up in friendships and family relationships, causing a strain on our marriage. Trauma and bullying had taught me I needed to save the world! It became a very present burden and informed the way I reacted to daily situations.

Eventually, my therapist said, "Brooke, you don't have to go around pushing people into holes. They'll fall in on their own!" A lightbulb moment for me! The focus needed to come back to me BEFORE I could help others. The urge to push people into holes and save the world was developed by the protective self that I referred to in Chapter 3. When we are operating out of the Protective Self, we find it safer to be right and in control and seek external validation from others.

ACHIEVING, NOT THRIVING

However, my answer to pain and eroded self-confidence from unhealthy relationships and tapes playing in my mind had always been to keep myself busy and achieve. If I could do something well and get external validation for it, it gave me a feeling of worthiness and value. So, I dove deep into a film project, *Fastlife,* to tell my husband's story of entering the world of professional motorsports. There were moments while I was developing *Fastlife* that stood out to me. One was when a woman who was working with my husband on social media content said something to me after I had created the trailer for the show. There was a line in my voiceover that said something like, "I was good at helping everyone else, even at the expense of myself." I didn't fully understand what she meant at the time, but she said, "Someday, you won't say that anymore." Just her saying that planted a seed and caused me to think that maybe this was part of the old foundation that needed to be removed. I just had no idea how to do it. When we set the intention to heal, the right people do come along, and usually, it's hindsight that allows us to see the key roles they play in our healing.

I worked and worked and worked. I worked for days, weeks, and months. I invested money and so much time into creating a TV show concept to sell to producers in Hollywood. I pushed, and I created. I pushed through all kinds of no's and criticisms and finally almost got a deal with a producer. I had hired a female lawyer from Hollywood, and she advocated for me. She found a sticking point in the contract and said, "If we can't get through this and he can't adjust something, this is a no-deal for you." I remember being on the conference call that day; I remember feeling intimidated but thankful I had her advocating for me. He didn't budge, and the deal didn't go through.

I didn't accept this as the end and kept pushing. I decided I would not give up. My husband's determination inspired me, and I was good at hard work and doing things for others. It did fulfill one desire, which was helping others do what they love to do, so I kept pushing. I prayed, too. Prayed and pushed! Eventually, we found a distributor who saw what we were trying to do with the project, and he offered to mentor me and help me get the show on Amazon Prime. He liked that we incorporated our faith into the show, and he thought our story could inspire people to live their dreams. So, I began one of the longest and hardest projects of my life, creating a ten-episode docuseries with all the footage I had filmed over the years. On and on I went, working day and night until we finally finished the product, and the show launched on Amazon in 2018.

I was riding high for a while, feeling accomplished, thinking, "Just you wait until I prove you wrong!" to all who didn't believe in me or tried to keep me in a box." My strength was increasing. The new walls were being built on a stronger foundation, but I didn't pace myself or check in with myself to honor how I was feeling. I was achieving, but it was still for some external validation. This prevented thriving, and I didn't know the difference. More than not thriving, I was exhausting myself. Additionally, one of our daughters was dealing with severe anxiety and OCD to the point that it was difficult for her to go to school. We were doing everything we could to help her, and it was hard to see her struggle. Our kids were feeling the stress, too, but at the time, it was hard to see the connection.

PHYSICAL MANIFESTATIONS OF A LIFETIME OF TRAUMA

One night, my husband was out of town, and I had gotten sick. I was very congested and didn't feel well at all, so I took some medicine and got into the bath. Within fifteen minutes, I felt so weird that I got up, stumbled out of the bathtub, and lay on the floor. I called for my daughter to help me. She did, and she was strong. She helped me get to the hospital. I was hardly able to walk. The only way to explain it was I felt like I was losing control of my body. I was cold and weak and didn't know what was happening.

My daughter and my mother-in-law took me to the hospital and stayed with me. My potassium was low, and I was really dehydrated. They treated me for that and released me. Derek wasn't supposed to be home for another day, and I was really scared. The next morning, I could hardly do anything, and I reached out to a couple of friends and family members while I waited for my husband to return home. I had never felt like I couldn't do anything, and I could barely go to the bathroom without feeling like I was going to pass out.

When my husband got home, we visited the doctor. He ran some tests, and it turned out that my thyroid had crashed, and I was diagnosed with hypothyroidism. I had always been healthy and able to do almost anything. My survival mode was to work and achieve. Not anymore. I was couch-bound. The doctor's orders were that Derek and the kids were to take over the cooking, laundry, and dishes, and I was to rest and recover. I had many visits to the doctor's office during this time. On one visit, the doctor asked me about my stress level and what could be going on for me emotionally. He was so kind and compassionate that this moment of him holding space for me brought tears to my eyes.

When I read the book *Whole Again,* this all made sense. MacKenzie delves into the profound connection between emotional trauma and its physical manifestations, emphasizing that the impact of psychological wounds is not confined to the mind alone but extends to the body.[22] The book articulates how trauma can translate into physical tension, chronic pain, and discomfort throughout various parts of the body. It explores the concept of psychosomatic symptoms, wherein emotional distress finds expression through bodily ailments such as digestive issues or unexplained pain. The intricate relationship between trauma and the nervous system is discussed, detailing how dysregulation can contribute to symptoms like panic attacks and chronic anxiety. Sleep disturbances, immune system suppression, and hypervigilance are also explored as tangible physical outcomes of prolonged exposure to trauma.

DISORDERED THINKING

Protective Self

Wound

---

22   Jackson MacKenzie, *Whole Again: Healing Your Heart and Rediscovering Your True Self after Toxic Relationships and Emotional Abuse* (Penguin Books, 2019).

When I read the book, I realized that my protective self, intertwined with my physical self, was exhausted! I recognized these bodily manifestations and began seeking a holistic approach to healing that encompasses both mental and physical well-being. Understanding the mind-body connection became a key component of the comprehensive healing journey I was on.

Not too long before, I had a good session with my therapist and a good cry. We identified that I had been holding in feelings about many things for a long time. One was a trauma my mom had when I was just four years old, how she coped with it and its residual effects on me as her daughter. When I was twelve, she shared with me what had happened, and I didn't really know how to process it. I would tell a couple of friends over the course of my school years, feeling the need to talk about it with someone and let it out, but they weren't prepared to talk about it or know what to say. So, I would stuff it back down again and feel a little vulnerable after sharing, and a bit of shame, too, for having what felt like such a heavy family secret.

So, on that day with the doctor, I mentioned I had this come up in therapy. I told him that, from time to time, when I felt safe with someone, I would have a profound cry and not be able to totally pinpoint what was coming to the surface or why I felt so sad. And he told me, "It's like you've been carrying this deep, dark secret for all these years, and it's finally coming into the light."

I began to cry, and it was a good one. It felt good to have that acknowledged. It felt nice to finally have permission to take a break and not work so hard, just survive. The doctor's orders were that I was to rest.

REST AND REFLECTION

And so, I got it. I was finally forced to slow down and rest. I had to ask a lot of my husband, and I had avoided being weak my whole life, so this was totally foreign to me. One day, I was reaching out in prayer and called a friend from church. She said, "God made you a masterpiece. How would you treat a masterpiece?" I'll never forget that, and since then, I've been so much better at caring for myself. It took me a good year or two to learn how and practice.

Challenges in life are our biggest gifts, and as soon as you can embrace them as such, your life changes dramatically. I was being given the gift of self-reflection time and the ability to have the time to become more self-aware. One book I truly found helpful was Louise Hay's book *You Can Heal Your Life*. As I read her words—humiliation, inadequacy, and feeling powerless—I nearly tipped over.[23] This described to a tee what I was feeling. I began working with her affirmations, specifically related to the thyroid.

"I move beyond old limitations and allow myself to express myself freely and creatively."

"I am always safe and secure. I trust the process of life."

"I love and approve of myself. I am free from all clutter and chaos."

Little by little, I felt little glimpses of freedom from the emotional heaviness and clutter I was living with. I began to understand the tie between my stored emotions and learned behavior patterns from trauma in the past and how it was manifesting in my body. I took the time to journal and reflect on my feelings and got better at being present in the moment. I didn't have the energy to forge ahead through every issue that arose at home or manage my husband and how he was parenting. I got to step back and allow him to lead more

---

23   Louise Hay, *You Can Heal Your Life* (HAY House INC, 2017).

because I physically couldn't. This allowed me to see that I often would jump in and fix things to avoid the anxiety of something left undone, which likely came from a feeling of not knowing how to process big feelings when I was young and feeling alone and targeted in my youth.

And since I was couch-bound and physically unable to move around very much for a while, I had lots of time and no excuses! No dishes to do, no people to take care of or save, no events to run off to. It was just me.

THE BENEFITS OF SELF-AWARENESS

Self-awareness is the capacity to look inward and understand our own feelings, emotions, stressors, and personality. These key understandings play a critical role in influencing our judgments, decisions, and interactions with others.

Self-awareness has many benefits, including:

- **Improved Emotional Intelligence:** Self-awareness can help you understand and manage your emotions better, leading to better decision-making, healthier relationships, and greater empathy toward others.
- **Increased Self-Confidence:** When you are self-aware, you have a clearer understanding of your strengths and weaknesses, allowing you to focus on your strengths and work on your weaknesses, leading to greater self-confidence.
- **Better Communication:** Self-awareness can help you understand your communication style and how it is perceived by others, leading to improved communication skills and more effective interactions with others.
- **Greater Personal Growth:** Being self-aware allows you to recognize patterns of behaviors or thoughts that may be holding you back and take steps to address them, leading to personal growth and development.

- **Enhanced Decision-Making:** With self-awareness, you can better understand your values, priorities, and goals, leading to more informed and intentional decision-making.

Self-awareness can lead to improved relationships, better personal and professional development, and a greater sense of fulfillment in life. Once I started to see this, I took time to journal about my values, desires, hopes, and fears.

As I healed, I started walking outside. I would do short walks and appreciate nature. The doctor prescribed therapeutic massage for me twice a month, a practice I still enjoy today. I would have never done that for myself had I not gone through this difficult physical setback. I changed my diet and ate healthy, nourishing foods. I began searching for ways to understand how I felt and to honor myself when my energy was low. I had a better barometer for when I would feel agitated, sad, upset, happy, or angry. I could catch myself early when I started feeling ramped up.

WHAT GOD SAYS ABOUT YOU

True love is really allowing yourself to explore your possibilities and what God has designed you for. The other part that was most important in my healing was looking beyond the physical experience to really understand my relationship with God and understanding more deeply what God says about me. I've always believed in God and feel a very strong connection to my Creator. When I was little, in Sunday school, we were taught that God is like the sun and we are His children connected to Him, just like rays of the sun. We express all the qualities of the Divine Creator, and we were made perfect in His image. Sometimes, I think this feels hard to live up to. I felt like if I made a mistake, I let God down and felt heaviness and guilt. But as I went through these hard things, I realized that the moment I would get on my knees and come back to my Creator and ask Him to lead, I would be led, and I would be fed with exactly the right support at the right time.

One of my favorite verses that I've come back to time and time again is:

> [11] For I know the plans I have for you, declares the LORD, plans for welfare and not for evil, to give you a future and a hope (Jeremiah 29:11).

I took this as a promise from an all-knowing and all-loving God that my future was filled with prosperity, and I was safe in God's hands right that instant. I held on to this for dear life! I began to see that my suffering was about my choices and not so much about being punished. As I began to value myself and look at myself as a ray of sunshine emanating out from God's infinite intelligence and goodness, I began to feel whole again. My body began to heal, and I was given opportunities to reframe my challenges and history into something that could not only help me heal, but possibly put me on a path to help others.

Another verse from over the years that has helped me, and a special teacher shared it with me, is 1 Peter 5:7: "Cast your cares (anxiety) upon him, for he cares for you." This Scripture helps us to know we can give our worries over to God. It helps us to realize that God does indeed care for us always.

WHAT I'VE LEARNED

> *While I had an awareness of ways in which I was broken and had accepted lies about myself, I didn't completely understand how it was hurting me or others yet. "This is how you get unstuck. You reach."*
> **Cheryl Strayed**

Some more digging was required, but I didn't get to it until I was forced to. And just like home projects, sometimes you find a new problem and must dig deeper to get to the foundational issue.

I learned so much from Louise Hay's book *You Can Heal Your Life*.[24] She explains that certain negative thought patterns and emotions can contribute to specific health problems. She suggests that thyroid issues may be related to feelings of humiliation, inadequacy, and feeling powerless. Hay suggests that if we are experiencing thyroid problems, we should examine our thoughts and emotions around these themes and work to release any negative patterns. This connected my experience with a therapist when one of our kids was dealing with anxiety and having trouble swallowing. The therapist said that anything with the throat relates to our ability to communicate our needs. She showed us how to help our daughter by gesturing from the throat area toward the mouth and saying at the same time, "What do you need to say?" This was to encourage her to speak her truth.

WHAT YOU CAN DO

A good first step is to thank the disappointment, even if you must curse it first! Anger is a secondary emotion. There is always a feeling to name beneath it; for example, I had a lot of sadness and loneliness. So then, why do we thank it? It is a way not to resist the lessons that come along with it. If I could thank the illness for giving me the gift of time to have self-awareness, then I would welcome the lessons.

I hope that by telling you my story, you might learn sooner to take the time to understand what is going on with your heart. Your emotional life and your physical life are inseparable. If you are struggling with an illness, relationships,

---

24   Louise Hay, *You Can Heal Your Life* (HAY House INC, 2017).

or have lost your way, God is as close as the air you breathe and, as my dad always said, "Lay it on the altar." Lay your problems and burdens down and allow God to care for you and take care of your concerns. If you are not sure about God or what you believe, look at a flower or a bug or any of the amazing creatures in nature and know that there is some kind of Creator working to create all this intricate beauty. There is a power outside us that you can surrender to.

My healing journey took at least a year. If you are just beginning, hang on! You can do this. When old emotional trauma resurfaces, it can feel like a dormant volcano suddenly erupting. Just like a volcano that has been quiet for years can suddenly spew hot lava and ash, emotional trauma that you thought was buried deep within can suddenly burst forth, overwhelming you with intense emotions and memories you thought were long gone. This can feel violent and chaotic, and you may feel you have no control over it. However, trust me, I know. Just like a volcano eventually settles down and becomes quiet again, with time and the right support, you can learn to process and heal from your emotional trauma.

Don't be pushed by your problems. Be led by your dreams.
Ralph Waldo Emerson

As you read this, if you are beginning to feel ready to explore what's going on in your heart and with your emotions, that's a good thing! If you feel triggered in any way, that's also a good thing. If you want to close the book, I challenge you to keep reading. Trust me, it's easy to run away, but in the long run, it's not easier. The termites in your walls will continue to eat and erode your structure. At some point, the walls will fall. I pray you can stop the problem before it destroys your dreams, hopes, and ability to be all that God created you to be.

REFLECTION QUESTIONS

Now it's time to focus a little more on journaling about where you find meaning and joy in your life. These questions are leading you toward the light and hopefully you are feeling lighter as you go through this process. Continue to stay open to exploring your heart and what you believe to be true. If you are left with questions, that's okay, too!

1. What causes you to be optimistic or pessimistic?
2. What makes you stressed or calm?
3. What are you thankful for today?
4. What makes your heart sing?
5. What big things are you most grateful for right now?
6. What does spirituality mean to you?
7. What do you believe makes the world a better place?
8. Do you believe you find your purpose, or does your purpose find you?
9. What gives your life meaning today?
10. What leaves you feeling purposeful?
11. What people or ideas have had the most significant impact on your spiritual life?
12. How do you define wisdom, and where do you look for wisdom in your own life?

ACTION STEP: DISCOVER YOUR STRENGTHS AND WEAKNESSES

- Ask five people you trust what you are good at, and what you could work on to determine some of your most prominent strengths and weaknesses. Take some time to journal on the reflection questions and what you discover about yourself from your trusted friends and family so you can gain clarity on your vision and who you want to become.

Chapter 6

CLARITY

The beauty is that through disappointment, you can gain clarity, and with clarity comes conviction and true originality.
Conan O'Brien

I am very good at being busy and working hard on projects that would seem to have a clear goal and purpose. I've learned along the way, however, that sometimes my hard work and busyness aren't exactly from a place of clarity; it's more anxious busywork with a sprinkle of my values mixed in. My husband is a race car driver, and I am a supporter. I go to almost all of his races; I don't miss one if I don't absolutely have to. I produced a show about his dream of driving race cars, and I hoped to inspire others to do the same. I created two seasons of ten episodes and accomplished getting them up on Amazon Prime. This was an incredible accomplishment, and I'd say it is something I am very proud of to this day.

He is now switching to a European racing series to race next year, and I've felt a nagging desire to film a documentary about his experience. I began going through all the footage and photos I have accumulated over the years and had a good laugh while reviewing what I have. The show was completed in 2018 and covered his racing journey between 2015 and 2017. I have literally never turned the camera off since then and have hundreds of hours of footage all the way through this last racing season in 2023.

There has been no clear plan to continue the show, and I suppose some of this footage could be used someday. However, half the time, I struggled to even enjoy being at the races because I was filming as if I couldn't miss the moment with no plan and no clarity about where anyone was going to watch all of this footage I was pouring myself into.

The reason I am sharing this with you is to remind you that it's good to take the time to get really clear on what you want to accomplish. This not only helps us keep our life in balance, but also allows us to create a clear action plan and make sure that what we are setting out to do aligns with our values and keeps us in balance with all the other areas of our lives.

ACCOUNTABILITY AND MOTIVATION

Working with a life coach can be a great way to gain clarity and stay accountable and motivated as you work toward your goals. The first time I called a coach, I didn't take the leap. Who knows, it might not have been the right one either. I arranged a call with her, and she shared with me all about mindset and how she could help me move out of this dark place. I remember feeling blown away by how expensive it was when she presented her prices, and coming from someone who couldn't even get herself to pay for therapeutic massage twice a week, asking for help that was costly and something I had never done before seemed like too much. So, I let it rest, but our conversation never left me. She recommended a book for me to read, so I did that, too. I was reading a lot and searching, but I still felt like I needed help.

One day, maybe a month or two later, when I was answering emails, I found a message from Tony Robbins about coaching. I signed up for a call and got set up with one of the Robbins organization coaches. I was apprehensive but open to trying it. I signed up for an entire year of coaching after that initial call. I took the leap, and I knew, at some level, there was more for me, but I didn't really know how to get there. I hoped this was the magic answer. I thought he would tell me what to do. I would tell him my problems, and poof! He would give me the step-by-step process to accomplish my goals.

I remember my first call with him. It was mainly me talking and him listening. I shared my story, a little reluctantly. I went through all my life experiences, and he quietly listened. He then asked me if I was ready for more. I wasn't sure what to do with this question yet, but I said, "Yes!" regardless. I later learned that coaches help you move forward to where you want to be, and a good coach won't let you stay stuck in the past. I was surprised at how comfortable I was sharing such personal details with someone I couldn't even see; it was all by phone. I was even more surprised that I was as comfortable as I was with a man, but I did have some concerns in the back of my mind about whether this would work.

I believe things happen for a reason, and looking back, I'm sure this was God's design. Here I was, talking to a healthy person, a man who was holding space for my emotions and who also had tools and ideas about how to move me more into the present and thinking about the future I wanted to create.

We worked together to identify the obstacles getting in the way of me accomplishing my goals. I learned that my social media use and worrying about others' opinions of me were just impeding what I had hoped to create. I learned I was a people-pleaser and that I needed to take steps to manage my boundaries better. I also learned that I had a pretty good idea of what I wanted to create, but no plan to get there yet.

We set clear goals, which helped me stay focused and motivated, and within a few short months, I stepped up to hire a business coach to help me launch a new website and blog. Right out of the gate, we worked with a coaching tool called the Triad. (More about this in Chapter 7.) This helped me understand emotions and how they affect my mental state. We began with tools to help me become aware of myself, my emotions, my actions, and the direction I wanted my life to go.

Six Human Needs

Out of this coaching, I learned many concepts and added plenty of tools to my life toolbox. One of these was learning about the Six Human Needs we all have. The Six Human Needs, as described by Tony Robbins, provide a comprehensive framework for understanding what drives human behavior and fulfillment. These needs encompass both our emotional and practical requirements for a meaningful life. The first four needs—certainty, variety, significance, and love/connection—are often referred to as the "personality needs" and are essential for our emotional well-being. We all seek a balance between the need for security (certainty) and the desire for novelty and excitement (variety). Significance drives our quest for a sense of importance, and love/connection forms the core of our relationships.

The last two needs—growth and contribution—are often known as the "spiritual needs" as they pertain to our personal development and the positive impact we make on others. The pursuit of growth and the joy of giving back help us find meaning and fulfillment in our lives. Recognizing and balancing these needs can be a powerful tool for personal development and improving the quality of our relationships and overall well-being.

This explained why I struggled to grow and contribute in the way I wanted to when I was in uncertain, and what I eventually learned were unhealthy, unsafe relationships. My personality needs could not be met while trying to find my significance in relationships with people who were so good at making me feel insignificant. I had to trade who I was and the values I believed in for love and connection to feel secure and certain. Hopefully, by now, if you are doing the same, you see that this is not a good deal for you. Just say "no" to trading your values to be accepted!

ELIMINATING DISTRACTIONS AND BEING MINDFUL

I learned how to be mindful and get quiet with my thoughts. I began trying meditation and working through what I needed to clarify about *Fastlife* and moving forward with my creative projects. This all came from getting quiet and meditating, and the ideas began to flow. I dipped my toe in the water by putting myself out there a little more and sharing more of my story on social media. I began curating my friends more intentionally and only doing things with people who were loving and supportive and minimized my time with people who were toxic.

Problems provide opportunities for growth. As we work through our issues and challenges, we gain new insights and develop new skills and strengths to overcome them. We then get to add these to our toolbox. Acknowledging that the problem will help us allows for a perspective shift to welcome the learning. By eliminating distractions and comparisons, you can focus your energy on your own growth and development and create a more fulfilling and purposeful life.

Here is a list of how you can eliminate distractions to make room for growth:

- **Identify Your Distractions:** The first step is to identify what is distracting you from your goals. This might include social media, email, TV shows, or even certain people in your life. Once you know what your distractions are, you can take steps to eliminate or reduce them.
- **Set Clear Goals:** When you work with a life coach, they can help you identify and set clear goals for yourself. This can help you stay focused and motivated and give you a sense of purpose and direction. Make sure your goals are specific, measurable, achievable, relevant, and time-bound (SMART), and work with your coach to create an action plan to achieve them.
- **Practice Mindfulness:** Mindfulness can help you stay focused and present in the moment, which can be especially helpful when you're feeling distracted or overwhelmed. Try practicing meditation or deep breathing exercises to calm your mind and help you stay centered.
- **Limit Your Social Media Use:** Social media can be a major source of distraction and comparison. Try setting limits on your social media use, such as only checking it once or twice a day or taking a break from it altogether for a set period.
- **Surround Yourself with Positive Influences:** Finally, surround yourself with people who support and encourage your personal growth and development. Avoid comparing yourself to others and instead focus on your own progress and accomplishments.

ARTIST DATES

While working with the coach, I reinstated an earlier practice I had read about. Doing "artist dates" was something I learned from a friend. Elizabeth Gilbert is a successful author who has written several bestselling books, including *Eat Pray Love*, *Big Magic: Creative Living Beyond Fear*, and *City of Girls*. It's difficult to say exactly what specific accomplishments she achieved because of doing artist dates, but it's clear that her commitment to nurturing her creativity and staying connected to her inner artist has been instrumental in her success.

In *Big Magic*, Gilbert talks about how the practice of doing artist dates helped her to generate new ideas and to stay open to the flow of creativity in her life.[25] By making a commitment to regular solo adventures that nourished her soul, she was able to tap into her imagination and generate new insights and inspiration.

PERSONALITY TESTING

Personality assessments are great to take at any stage of life. Don't be hard on yourself if you are entering a phase of life where you feel like you should be farther along with your self-awareness. Traditional education systems often prioritize academic subjects and skill development, leaving little room for teaching emotional intelligence and self-awareness. In some cultures, discussing emotions and self-awareness may not be as common or encouraged, which can limit opportunities for children to develop these skills.

Parents and caregivers play a significant role in a child's upbringing. If they are not well-versed in self-awareness and emotional intelligence, they may not prioritize teaching these

---

25   Elizabeth Gilbert, *Big Magic Creative Living beyond Fear* (New York: Penguin Random House Audio, 2015).

skills to their children. We are only able to share the tools we have. Teaching self-awareness can be challenging as it requires the development of a child's emotional and introspective skills, which are complex and may not be fully developed until later stages of cognitive and emotional development. The importance of self-awareness and emotional intelligence has gained more recognition in recent years. Consequently, there is a growing movement to incorporate these skills into educational curricula and parenting practices.

Self-awareness is one of the underrated superpowers in life, allowing us to understand ourselves better, make informed decisions, and interact more effectively with others. It is a fundamental component of emotional intelligence. People who are self-aware can recognize and understand their own emotions, which enables them to manage their feelings more effectively. This, in turn, leads to better self-control, empathy, and social skills.

Self-aware individuals are more likely to make decisions that align with their values, goals, and desires. They have a clearer understanding of their strengths and weaknesses, which helps them make choices that lead to personal and professional growth. Self-awareness can lead to more harmonious and productive relationships. When people understand their own triggers, biases, and communication styles, they can adapt and relate to others more effectively, fostering empathy and connection.

Self-awareness is a key driver of personal growth. It allows individuals to identify areas for improvement and to actively work on their weaknesses, as well as emphasize their strengths and leverage them. This continuous self-improvement can lead to a more fulfilling and purpose-driven life. It can help individuals build resilience. When they understand how they react to adversity and stress, they can develop coping strategies to bounce back more quickly from setbacks. Additionally, self-aware individuals tend to live more authentically. They are in touch with their values and beliefs, making it easier for them to live a life that aligns with their true selves.

I found it helpful to do the following personality tests and assessments to gain better self-awareness. I dug into really understanding what made me tick. I began to understand why I did things the way I did by taking the tests and then reading about what careers I would be good at, what strengths I had, what tendencies I had, and how my type tends to respond in relationships.

The Enneagram

The Enneagram can be a valuable tool in life due to its ability to foster self-awareness and personal growth. By identifying your Enneagram type, you gain insights into your core motivations, fears, and behaviors, allowing you to understand yourself and your tendencies better. This knowledge serves as a foundation for making informed life choices, cultivating healthier relationships, and improving communication with others. It can guide you in setting meaningful goals, managing stress, and ultimately, lead you to a more balanced and fulfilling life. With the Enneagram's help, individuals can embark on a journey of self-discovery, self-improvement, and the development of empathy and understanding for the diversity of human experiences, enhancing both personal and interpersonal aspects of their lives.

Taking the Enneagram personality test can be beneficial in several ways, as it can provide you with insights into your personality, motivations, and behaviors. Here are some ways in which taking the Enneagram test can help you in life:

- **Self-Awareness:** The Enneagram system identifies nine core personality types, each with its own set of motivations, fears, and desires. By understanding your Enneagram type, you gain valuable insights into your own thought patterns, behaviors, and tendencies. This increased self-awareness can help you make more informed choices in various aspects of your life.

- **Personal Growth:** Once you've identified your Enneagram type, you can explore the associated traits and tendencies. This knowledge can serve as a starting point for personal growth and self-improvement. You can work on overcoming unhealthy patterns and developing your strengths, ultimately leading to a more balanced and fulfilling life.
- **Improved Relationships:** The Enneagram can also help you understand the motivations and behaviors of others. By recognizing the Enneagram types of your friends, family members, and coworkers, you can gain insight into their perspectives, needs, and communication styles. This can lead to more empathetic and effective interpersonal relationships.
- **Conflict Resolution:** Understanding your Enneagram type and the types of others can be particularly useful in resolving conflicts. It allows you to see the underlying motivations and fears that may be driving the disagreement, making it easier to find common ground and work toward a resolution.
- **Career and Life Choices:** Your Enneagram type can offer guidance when it comes to career and life decisions. It can help you identify your strengths, weaknesses, and core values, making it easier to choose a path that aligns with your true self and brings you fulfillment.
- **Stress Management:** The Enneagram system also describes how each type responds to stress and what behaviors they might exhibit when under pressure. Recognizing your stress patterns can help you proactively manage stress and avoid unhealthy coping mechanisms.
- **Increased Empathy and Compassion:** As you learn about the different Enneagram types, you develop a deeper

understanding of the diverse ways people experience the world. This knowledge can lead to increased empathy and compassion, as you recognize that everyone has their own unique set of challenges and motivations.

- **Enhanced Communication:** Knowing your Enneagram type and the types of those around you can improve communication. It enables you to tailor your message and approach to the preferences and needs of the other person, making conversations more effective and less likely to lead to misunderstandings.
- **Goal-Setting and Personal Development:** With an understanding of your Enneagram type, you can set more meaningful and achievable goals. This knowledge can help you prioritize personal development areas and work toward a sense of wholeness and self-actualization.

Once I knew my Enneagram type and the types of my family members, it really helped me to understand what makes them tick and what I thrive on. We also found some humor in how some of the relationship suggestions perfectly matched our types. The areas where we got stuck were almost exactly areas that the Enneagram stated were weak points or things that didn't work well for our types. Once you understand yourself better, you stop thinking that you need to be like everyone else and you understand that each of us is unique, with different needs and tendencies.

It's important to note that the Enneagram is just one tool among many for personal development and understanding personality. While it can offer valuable insights, it should be used in conjunction with other methods and self-discovery techniques for a more comprehensive understanding of oneself and others.

For more information about the Enneagram Personality Test, visit https://www.enneagraminstitute.com/.

Myers-Briggs

The first personality test I took is one of the originals. The Myers-Briggs Type Indicator (MBTI) personality test, developed by Katharine Cook Briggs and her daughter Isabel Briggs Myers in the mid-20th century, has a rich history in the field of psychology. Rooted in the work of Carl Jung, the MBTI was designed to provide individuals with a practical and accessible way to understand and categorize their personality preferences. By assessing key dimensions such as extraversion vs. introversion, sensing vs. intuition, thinking vs. feeling, and judging vs. perceiving, the MBTI helps people gain a deeper understanding of their natural inclinations and decision-making processes.

Understanding your MBTI type can be a powerful tool for self-discovery and personal growth. It can shed light on your communication style, problem-solving methods, and how you interact with others. This knowledge can enhance self-awareness, improve relationships, and inform career choices, ultimately enabling individuals to make more informed and fulfilling life decisions by aligning them with their core personality preferences.

I particularly liked the Myers Briggs testing because it not only helped me understand myself better but also provided a list of potentially fitting career choices. It also gives information about your type in relationships and communication style, which I think are helpful to point you in some direction for further self-exploration and careers to try.

For more information about the Myers-Briggs Type Indicator personality test, visit https://www.themyersbriggs. com/.

CliftonStrengths

As a coach now, I understand the importance of clients focusing on their strengths to leverage them to overcome challenges and accomplish goals in their lives. Years ago, I found The Strengths Finder book which included a test to identify your top three strengths. The StrengthsFinder test, also known as the Clifton Strengths assessment, is designed to help individuals discover and understand their natural strengths and talents. Here's how the StrengthsFinder test can assist you in understanding your strengths:

- **Self-Awareness:** The test provides a list of your top strengths or talents based on your responses to the assessment questions. This insight allows you to become more aware of your unique qualities and abilities. It helps you identify what you naturally excel at and what energizes you.
- **Emphasis on Strengths:** Unlike some personality assessments that focus on weaknesses or areas for improvement, the StrengthsFinder test places its primary emphasis on identifying and leveraging your strengths. This positive approach encourages you to build on your existing strengths, which can lead to greater self-confidence and overall well-being.
- **Personalized Insights:** Each person's StrengthsFinder results are unique. By understanding your specific strengths, you can gain insights into your preferred ways of thinking, feeling, and acting. This knowledge can help you make more informed choices in various areas of your life.
- **Career and Personal Development:** The StrengthsFinder test is often used in career development and personal growth. Knowing your strengths can guide you in selecting the right career, choosing the best roles within a

team, and making decisions about your educational and professional path. It can also inform your approach to personal development, helping you set goals that align with your innate talents.

- **Improved Relationships:** Understanding your strengths can enhance your interactions with others. When you appreciate your own strengths and those of others, you can build more effective relationships. You can collaborate more productively, delegate tasks based on strengths, and navigate conflicts with a greater understanding of each person's unique contributions.
- **Goal Setting:** With the knowledge of your strengths, you can set more meaningful and achievable goals. Whether in your career, personal life, or hobbies, aligning your goals with your strengths can increase your chances of success and fulfillment.
- **Empowerment:** Discovering your strengths through the StrengthsFinder test can empower you to be more authentic and confident. Embracing and using your strengths allows you to perform at your best and lead a more satisfying and purpose-driven life.
- **Continuous Learning and Improvement:** While the StrengthsFinder test reveals your inherent strengths, it doesn't mean you should neglect areas that require development. It encourages ongoing self-improvement by acknowledging that everyone has the capacity to build new skills and develop in other areas as well.

The StrengthsFinder test is a valuable tool for gaining self-awareness and understanding your strengths. It enables you to build on your innate talents, make informed choices, and lead a more fulfilling life by leveraging your strengths in various aspects of your personal and professional life.

For more information about the StrengthsFinder test, visit https://www.gallup.com/cliftonstrengths/.

DISC

Finally, since I have received coaching training from the Robbins Madanes group, I have found the DISC assessment that I now use with clients to help them understand themselves better. Tony Robbins, a renowned motivational speaker and self-help guru, has used various tools and assessments, including the DISC assessment, as part of his coaching and personal development programs. The reason he incorporates the DISC assessment, like many other coaches and professionals, is to help individuals gain self-awareness and improve their personal and professional lives.

The DISC assessment is a psychological tool that helps individuals gain a better understanding of themselves and their interpersonal behaviors. It is based on a theory developed by psychologist William Marston and expanded upon by others. The DISC assessment measures four primary personality traits, each represented by a letter:

- **Dominance (D):** This trait focuses on assertiveness, control, and a tendency to take charge in situations. Individuals with a high "D" score are often seen as direct, competitive, and results-oriented.
- **Influence (I):** The "I" trait revolves around sociability, enthusiasm, and the desire to influence or persuade others. People with a strong "I" tendency are often outgoing, persuasive, and social.
- **Steadiness (S):** The "S" trait emphasizes patience, cooperation, and a preference for stability and harmony in relationships. Individuals high in "S" are typically dependable, loyal, and supportive.
- **Conscientiousness (C):** The "C" trait is about precision, attention to detail, and a focus on quality and accuracy. Those with a strong "C" characteristic tend to be organized, analytical, and systematic.

The DISC assessment can help you understand yourself better in the following ways:

- **Self-Awareness:** By identifying your primary DISC traits, you can gain insight into your natural tendencies and behaviors in different situations. This awareness can help you recognize your strengths and areas for improvement.
- **Communication:** Understanding your DISC profile can improve your communication skills. It allows you to tailor your communication style to better connect with others who have different personality traits, enhancing interpersonal relationships.
- **Conflict Resolution:** Recognizing the DISC profiles of others can help you understand their communication preferences and conflict-resolution styles. This knowledge can be valuable in resolving disputes and building more harmonious relationships.
- **Career and Work Dynamics:** The DISC assessment can provide guidance on choosing a career that aligns with your personality traits. It can also help in identifying the types of roles and work environments that are a good fit for you.
- **Personal Development:** Once you understand your DISC profile, you can work on strengthening certain traits or adapting your behavior in situations that may require a different approach. This can contribute to personal growth and a more well-rounded personality.

The DISC assessment is a useful tool for increasing self-awareness, improving communication, and enhancing your understanding of how your personality traits influence your behavior and interactions with others. It can be especially helpful in various aspects of life, from career choices to building better relationships.

For more information on the DISC assessment, visit https://www.tonyrobbins.com/disc/.

While self-awareness may not always be explicitly taught to children, it's an essential life skill that can be cultivated and nurtured at any age. Parents, educators, and individuals themselves can work to promote self-awareness through open conversations, role-modeling, and the introduction of mindfulness practices, ultimately equipping children with a superpower that can benefit them throughout their lives. A life coach can be a wonderful facilitator for developing and honing some of these skills.

As I worked through my life challenges, I realized I lacked self-awareness and began an adventure in understanding myself. Stay curious, and don't give up! We are all learning and growing all the time.

FOCUS

As I worked with my coach and developed a more specific plan for my future, I noticed where my energy vampires lived. This is anything or anyone who sucks you dry and leaves you feeling like a deflated balloon afterward. Since we are creatures of habit, we can fall into the trap of heavily focusing on what's not working well in relationships or life. What happens when you focus on a problem? You tend to find more problems, not solutions. Instead, it's better to plan and focus on the outcome. There is a proverb that says, "If you don't have a plan for yourself, you'll be part of someone else's."

One famous person who set a clear intention to do something and created and followed a plan to get there was Oprah Winfrey. Oprah is a media executive, talk show host, actress, and philanthropist. She grew up in poverty in rural Mississippi and faced many challenges throughout her life, including abuse and discrimination.

Despite these challenges, Oprah developed a strong work ethic and a clear vision of what she wanted to achieve. She created a plan to become a successful television personality and worked tirelessly to achieve her goals. She started out as a local news anchor and eventually became the host of her own talk show, *The Oprah Winfrey Show*, which became one of the highest-rated programs in television history.

Oprah's success was due in large part to her ability to follow a plan. She set clear goals, broke them down into smaller steps, and worked diligently to achieve each one. She also had a strong support system, including mentors and advisors, who helped her stay on track and make strategic decisions.

Today, Oprah is one of the most influential and successful women in the world, with a net worth of over $3.5 billion.[26] Her success is a testament to the power of setting goals and following a well-designed plan to achieve them.

What I've Learned

Working with a life coach helped me gain clarity on my goals. There weren't any magic pills given, but I did find answers as I went through the process. I was also committed for a year, and each time we met, every two weeks, we would determine actions I would take to move me toward the future I wanted to create. My masterpiece was in preparation for its unveiling. I am writing this book today because I wrote it in my vision plan.

I had to take the leap and have the courage to ask for help and sign up with a publisher to get it done, but the first step was to craft the vision and make sure I wrote it down in my plan. I then needed to focus on where I wanted to

---

26   MSN, accessed September 27, 2023, https://www.msn.com/en-us/entertainment/entertainment-celebrity/what-is-oprah-winfrey-s-net-worth-in-2023/.

go instead of all the distractions of my daily life that like to arise to throw me off. Even if I have an off day, I make it a practice to revisit my vision and goals to ground myself in where I am headed and what I can do right now to move in that direction.

One of the biggest things from working with a coach was the practice of honoring myself and my time and allowing for dedicated time to work on just me. For a recovering people-pleaser, this was a very good thing. For most of my life, I would sacrifice my health and peace to do for others. This is where I began learning this was not sustainable or wise. Remember when Gail said, "One day, you won't say that anymore." That day had come!

Perhaps your day is coming, too? I think so! Let's do this.

What You Can Do

Clarity is power because we run with patterns. Bring your vision closer and closer so you can taste it. Additionally, it's time to remember LOYT, another key acronym I learned in Unleash Her Power Within.[27] It stands for "live life on your terms." You are the curator of the masterpiece of your life, layer by layer, creating and crafting your vision. The time dedicated to this will not leave you where it found you, and you will not be disappointed if you keep at it. So, what could possibly hold you back now that you have everything clear? Let's anticipate the challenges ahead so that we can answer them with gusto!

Tony Robbins says, "Where your focus goes, energy flows." What about doing a focus audit and just taking notes throughout the day of what you are focused on? One example of how "where we put our focus, our energy goes" is the metaphor of a garden. Having a clear picture of the past

---

27   Karissa Kouchis, "Unleash Her Power Within – Powered by Tony Robbins," accessed December 7, 2023, https://uhpw.com/.

and what you've been through is a vital step to healing if you don't stay there. The mind is like a sponge, and through the years of bullying and abuse, being left out, called names, and told you are not good enough can create a stacking effect that erodes your God-given awareness of your wholeness. It is so important to understand it fully, but then understand who you really are.

Just like a garden, our lives need consistent attention and effort to thrive. If we focus our attention on nurturing the soil, planting and watering the seeds, pulling out the weeds, and providing enough sunlight and nutrients, we will see our garden flourish and grow. Similarly, if we focus our energy on positive thoughts, healthy habits, and meaningful goals, we are more likely to achieve success and happiness in our lives. On the other hand, if we allow negativity, distractions, and self-doubt to take root in our minds, we may find ourselves feeling stuck and unfulfilled.

In both cases, the outcomes we experience are directly related to where we choose to focus our attention and energy. You can't pull the weeds from the garden when they are all mixed in with the producing plants. If you try to make sweeping changes and dig it all up at once, you'll lose the entire thing and the lessons learned. This is why I emphasized telling the whole story. Just imagine what you could create if you allowed your life to be like a well-tended garden! Our earlier metaphor of rebuilding a house can apply here, too. This is the step that happens before you begin the rebuild. You've investigated the structural weaknesses, and you've researched all that's necessary to create a strong foundation and structure to build on now. The next step is to create a clear vision for your garden, home, and masterpiece—that is you!

REFLECTION QUESTIONS

Creating a vision for your life is a powerful way to set clear goals and aspirations. To begin, take some quiet, focused time to reflect on what you want your life to look like in the future. By contemplating these questions, you can create a meaningful and purpose-driven vision for your life.

1. What are your core values and beliefs?
2. What brings you joy and fulfillment?
3. What impact do you want to make on the world?
4. Where do you see yourself in 5, 10, or 20 years?
5. What are your strengths and passions?
6. How do you want to balance your personal and professional life?
7. What kind of relationships do you want to nurture?
8. What legacy do you want to leave behind?
9. How can you align your vision with your daily actions and decisions?
10. If you could do anything without limits, what would it be?

ACTION STEP: 15-MINUTE VISION BOARD PROJECT

This project serves as a powerful tool for manifesting your goals, as the act of selecting and arranging images and words associated with your aspirations can reinforce your commitment to achieving them. By regularly viewing your vision board, you can stay focused on your objectives, maintain motivation, and even find creative solutions to make your dreams a reality. Whether you're seeking clarity on your goals or looking for an enjoyable and time-effective way to stay inspired, the 15-Minute Vision Board Project is a great starting point for visualizing your future.

It's a quick and inspiring exercise that involves gathering images, words, and visuals that represent your dreams, desires, and ambitions. In just 15 minutes, you'll create a visual collage that encapsulates your vision for various aspects of your life, such as career, relationships, health, personal growth, and more. Set a timer, clip pictures from magazines, and place them on a board. Allow yourself the freedom to not overthink it and just place on the board what speaks to you in this time window.

I have created both physical vision boards and digital ones. If you need an example, see below for an example of a digital vision board I created in January for the upcoming year.

CHAPTER 7

WHY WE DON'T GROW

Most everything you want is just outside of your comfort zone.
Jack Canfield

O ver the years, I have spent a lot of time hanging around with people that didn't have my best interest at heart, not necessarily because they were bad people, but because they were not a fit at that time in my life. I've shared a lot about bullying in my younger years and decisions I made in college that were not aligned with my values and life path. When I was a young mom, I moved to Southern Oregon, five hours away from where I grew up. I moved to a small town and had a baby, and was very anxious about fitting in and being part of a new family and a social group. I tried really hard to be everything everyone else wanted me to be.

I walked into a friend group that was my husband's social group he had years of connection with and I tried so hard to be part of it and for the friendships to grow. I was afraid of screwing it up, so sometimes I wasn't always truthful about things that weren't working and so much energy was going out that I lost myself in it. I wasn't working as hard with my own family that I moved away from and some of my friends from the past. I was the first one to have a child so emotionally and physically I was in a bit of a different realm with my life and it was sometimes hard to connect and feel like I fit in.

Derek and I would argue frequently about how much time to spend with friends versus nurturing our own new family and what to do to please our family. I developed severe anxiety and started having panic attacks. At one point, I was barely functioning and had to rely heavily on Derek to calm me when one would come up. Often they would arise when we'd be out to dinner with friends or family in large groups. I'd begin to feel panicky and lightheaded and then, before I knew it, I would feel completely out of control of my body and my mind. I even thought at one point I was having a heart attack.

We worked with a family physician that later shared with me that when you are feeling anxious like this, it is our body flashing a warning light at us that something is out of alignment. At the time, I was in it so I couldn't exactly identify what it was, but I did reach out for some therapy help. As I began to unpack my emotions and take the time to understand what was triggering the anxiety, I realized that I was expending so much energy outside of myself, trying to please others and fit in and do things that were expected of me AND on top of it learn how to raise a new baby as a new mom, that I wasn't able to focus on my heart and what was going to be aligned with my values. My warning system was telling me I was out of alignment and not looking where I wanted to go.

I grew up waterskiing and wakeboarding. In college, I was on the water ski team. The leading rule was to look where you wanted to go. If I was attempting to master the slalom course at a new speed, the rule was to not look at the buoys you were skiing around but to look to the trees on that side. Keep your head up and look past where you want to go. If you looked at the buoy, you would come up short every time. If you looked up and beyond the buoy, you would make it around the buoy and onto the next one. Now, attempting to learn a 360 on the wake surfboard, the lesson is the same. Turn your head in the direction you want to go; don't look down at the water or some other way. Look where you want to go!

The same goes for goals and dreams. You must clarify where it is you are headed and what your values are (including your standards), or you'll end up with whatever the standards are of those around you. If you are lucky, they are good for you, but often, the standards of others may not be what you want in life. That can only come from you, your heart, and what God placed there.

SETTING THE COURSE FOR YOUR LIFE

I heard this perspective somewhere, "No means 'go,' and fail means 'sail!'" Some people reframe roadblocks and obstacles as "teachers" and "trainers." I wouldn't be writing this book if I hadn't had so many hard things happen. At one point, I worked with someone on my social media, and she said, "Wow, you've really been through it." I almost have needed consistent reminders from outside of me to acknowledge what has happened. Your perspective is key to your healing success. Shannon L. Alder wrote the following six beliefs that set the course of your life:

1. If you don't believe the impossible can happen, then you are right.
2. When you feel like you are less than others, then you are right.
3. When you believe what you have and how you were raised keeps you from having everything you ever dreamed of, you are right.

4. When you believe your mistakes can't be undone, you are right.
5. When you feel this is the best it will ever get, you are right.
6. When you think someone will never change or rise above their brokenness, you are WRONG!"

And here's another perspective shocker for you. This may even sound insensitive at first. Tony Robbins says, "Life is happening FOR YOU." If you've been bullied, this sounds almost silly at first. It may even evoke some feelings, perhaps a little anger. If you've been sexually assaulted, raped, kicked around, beaten up, shamed, or told you were no good or unlovable, it's probably hard to see life as happening "for you." But what if it truly is? How can we come to accept this perspective?

Let's take the example of a young woman who has been the victim of unwanted sexual advances or, like me, a girl on the beach minding her business and then being threatened with physical harm by a crowd of older kids. I've witnessed one of these, and my friend in college was sexually assaulted at a college party. In both cases, a choice was made to heal from these horrible situations. In both cases, we reached out for help, found our strength through processing our pain and overcoming the shame and feelings that came with it and grew into stronger people. Yes, they were forceful situations against our will where we were violated, but did they ultimately push us to find our strength and grow? Fortunately, in both cases, the choice was made to survive and learn how to thrive again. We can shift our perspective to holding onto the idea that *life is happening for us.*

UNDERSTANDING BELIEFS

Our beliefs guide our perspective, identity, thoughts, feelings, words, actions, habits, values, and destiny. It's helpful to understand the difference between a limiting belief and an empowering belief and how we accumulate these beliefs. Limiting beliefs are beliefs that hold us back, create self-doubt, and prevent us from reaching our full potential, while empowering beliefs are beliefs that encourage us, build confidence, and motivate us to take positive action. Empowering beliefs are transformative, supportive beliefs that we can consciously choose and adopt so that we can create our best life of joy, purpose, meaning, fulfillment, harmony, abundance, and impact.

The movie *Inside Out is* a kids' movie by Pixar that explores the themes of the human mind and emotions. The setting takes place inside the mind of an eleven-year-old girl named Riley, where her emotions—Joy, Sadness, Anger, Fear, and Disgust—are personified as characters. The story follows Joy and Sadness as they embark on a journey through Riley's mind, trying to find their way back to the control center after getting lost in the maze of memories. Along the way, the movie highlights the importance of each emotion and how they work together to shape a person's thoughts, actions, and memories. In this film, we learn about the complexities of the human mind and the imprinted emotions that occur when certain experiences happen in our lives. When something is imprinted on these neural pathways, it plays like a tape repeatedly, informing our actions and decisions. They then become patterns and can fill us with limiting beliefs, preventing us from becoming the best versions of ourselves.

IDENTIFY YOUR LIMITING BELIEFS

You also have experiences that imprint certain beliefs on you and create these neural pathway tapes that run by default, and they become how you respond and, often, react to things. Our mind is like a computer; it has neuropathways. Much of what we do is directed by our subconscious mind and these neural pathways. They become the tapes that play, and the emotions are tied into the experiences.

Here are some steps you can take to separate limiting beliefs from empowering beliefs:

- **Identify Your Beliefs:** Start by identifying your beliefs about yourself, your abilities, and the world around you. Write them down and be as specific as possible.
- **Evaluate Each Belief:** For each belief, ask yourself whether it empowers you or limits you. Does it help you achieve your goals, or does it hold you back?
- **Look for Evidence:** Evaluate each belief based on evidence. Ask yourself if the belief is based on facts or just assumptions. If the belief is not supported by evidence, it may be a limiting belief.
- **Check for Consistency:** Look for consistency in your beliefs. If you hold conflicting beliefs, it can lead to confusion and indecision. Identify the beliefs that are consistent with your goals and values.
- **Challenge Your Limiting Beliefs:** Once you've identified your limiting beliefs, challenge them. Ask yourself if they are true. Try to find evidence to support or refute them. Replace your limiting beliefs with empowering beliefs. Take your top three limiting beliefs and write an affirmation to put that B.S. down! Post it on a mirror you look in daily.
- **Practice Your Empowering Beliefs:** Once you've identified your empowering beliefs, practice them.

Repeat them to yourself often. Visualize yourself acting on them and achieving your goals.

If you are operating out of your subconscious and cannot identify these and process the experiences that shaped them, you will likely feel like life is happening to you all the time. You will feel like a victim of your own mind and emotions. I know because, over and over, I would repeatedly react to certain situations in a specific way, producing the same result. There's one that stands out to me that I can use as an example.

I was working on a film project with a friend. This was a guy about my age. He suggested we do something on the project, and I took it as he was dominating me and controlling the project. I snapped at him, accusing him of being controlling. While I don't remember the exact details of the disagreement, I do remember how I was stopped in my tracks and never forgot what he said next.

"I am not that kind of guy. You have me all wrong."

His response jarred me, immediately quieted me, and made me realize something. It was said with kindness and sincerity, and I suddenly realized I was responding to him as if he was one of my past toxic relationships, and I was auto-responding to protect myself. I was in survival mode. I believed at that moment that something was happening to me and I needed to fight when, truthfully, he was just making a suggestion. I could have said politely, "This doesn't work for me," or invited a discussion on the topic. This story illustrates the importance of separating limiting beliefs from empowering beliefs.

REAL-WORLD STORIES OF OVERCOMING LIMITING BELIEFS

Empowering beliefs can sometimes inspire us to strive for heights we may not have reached otherwise. And it's an important lesson for those who are navigating the sometimes difficult journey of growth. It's important to know that some of the most successful people in the world have overcome tremendous obstacles, including bullying, to reach their goals. These are inspiring people who have accomplished their goals despite their own specific obstacles. They all seem to have developed a knack for facing challenges as well as the necessary grit to keep moving forward and overcome their limiting beliefs from childhood bullying experiences.

Inocente

This film documents the personal and vibrant coming-of-age story about a young artist's determination never to surrender to the bleakness of her surroundings.[28] At fifteen, Inocente refuses to let her dream of becoming an artist be caged by being an undocumented immigrant forced to live homeless for the last nine years. Color is her personal revolution, and its sweep on her canvases creates a world that looks nothing like her own dark past. *Inocente* is both a timeless story about the transformative power of art and a timely snapshot of the new face of homelessness in America: children. The challenges are staggering, but the hope in her story proves that the hand she has been dealt does not define her; her dreams do.

Nick Vujicic

Growing up in Melbourne, Australia, Nick Vujicic was born with no arms and legs and struggled mentally, emotionally, and physically.[29] Bullied at school, he attempted suicide when he was just ten years old by trying to drown himself

---

28 "Inocente," Rocky Mountain Women's Film, August 28, 2019, https://rmwfilm.org/films/inocente/.

29 "Dis-Arming Nick," Nick Vujicic, accessed September 27, 2023, https://nickvujicic.com/.

in a bathtub. Eventually, coming to terms with his disability, Nick decided to become vocal about living with disabilities and finding hope and meaning in life.

Elon Musk

Born in Pretoria, South Africa, Elon was bullied by schoolmates for being the smallest and youngest in his school.[30] These weren't casual bullies who just teased. He needed to recuperate in a hospital after a group of boys pushed him down a flight of stairs, causing him to black out. After he fell, the boys beat him mercilessly.

During his time at school, bullied kids had to continue to attend classes while facing their tormentors daily. Musk hated it, becoming lonely and withdrawn. Even in the most severe cases of bullying, there are places of refuge and saviors who help. Elon looked first to his family. An unusual group, they had a long history of breaking barriers and achieving the impossible, being both wanderers and adventurers throughout the generations. Another refuge that opened doors to his future was computers. He is also a born entrepreneur.

Today, Elon Musk is one of the wealthiest businessmen in the world. He's a high-tech entrepreneur aiming for the stars and tomorrow's automobile line. Elon is a world-renowned entrepreneur, CEO, and founder of companies such as SpaceX, Tesla, and Neuralink.

Catherine (Kate) Middleton

Kate began school as a first-year secondary student at Downe House, a well-known girls' boarding school in Berkshire,

---

30 "Elon Musk: From Bullied Schoolboy to World's Richest Man," The Guardian, January 7, 2021, https://www.theguardian.com/technology/2021/jan/07/elon-musk-from-bullied-schoolboy-to-worlds-richest-man.

England.[31] She started at Downe House at thirteen years of age rather than eleven, so most of the other students had a two-year head start in making friends and settling in. Also, Kate wasn't a boarder but a day pupil, living at her parents' home. She missed nightly bonding and social activities, putting her at a disadvantage.

She'd been a star of the field hockey team in primary school, but at Downe, they played lacrosse, where Kate didn't successfully make the switch. Kate Middleton just didn't fit in well at the cliquey school. She was ignored and teased, while the staff suggested she just "ignore the pain and carry on."

Kate did indeed. She carried on to a far more suited experience for her, transferring to St. Andrews Prep. She is now the wife of the future King of England, Prince William, mother to three children, and a valued member of the Royal Family. Her Royal Highness, the Duchess of Cambridge, is a member of the British Royal Family, a mother, and a philanthropist.

Padma Lakshmi

Padma Lakshmi was born in Chennai, India, and grew up in the United States. When she was in school, she was the target of bullying girls. "One time somebody crushed an egg on my head and punched [me] in the face—it was horrible. I used to be called giraffe [because of her 5'10" height], and it just makes you feel so, so alone and so scared."

Those days are now long behind her as the natural beauty has been in the public eye for more than twenty years as a TV

---

31 Majid Alam, "Princess Kate was 'Bullied Badly' at School, Here's How It Had a Huge Impact on Her Parenting," MSN, June 14, 2023, https://www.msn.com/en-in/news/world/princess-kate-was-bullied-badly-at-school-here-s-how-it-had-a-huge-impact-on-her-parenting/ar-AA1cxHuu?ocid=socialshare.

host, model, author, and activist, always finding time in her heart for other bullied girls. Padma is a supermodel, cooking host, and writer who blends the cultures of India and the US.

Moving Away from the Painful and Look at What You Want to Build

As humans, we are an accumulation of patterns of responding to what happens to us. When we decide to change, something happens. We begin developing an awareness of our patterns, but we aren't instantly changed into the person we want to become. It takes practice. Just like you wouldn't expect to become a world-class athlete with zero training, you cannot become who you want to be without some effort into awareness, understanding your triggers, patterns, choices, and why you make them, and the emotional root of why you do any of it.

Once you have this awareness, then you must create the vision for who you want to become and begin applying it. As you do this, you'll slip up from time to time. I have had many slips, but a common mistake people make when they have a misstep is to go off the rails, be hard on themselves, and give up. It's totally normal if this has happened to you. I had a total lightbulb moment when I took the course Unleash Her Power Within with Karissa Kouchis, and she taught us that as quickly as we catch that we are slipping back into old habits or patterns, we can do something to trigger our system to remember who we want to become and immediately shift.[32] This lifted a tremendous amount of guilt off of my shoulders when I learned this because I was judging myself in an all-or-nothing system and weighing myself down with feeling bad that I kept messing up.

---

32   Karissa Kouchis, "Unleash Her Power Within – Powered by Tony Robbins," accessed December 7, 2023, https://uhpw.com/.

Now I can catch it, sometimes even find humor in it, own it, and move on!

THE TRIAD

A coaching tool I often use with my clients is called the "Triad." This was one of the first things I learned about while working with a life coach. My coach shared with me a quote that I constantly use now by Tony Robbins: "Where focus goes, energy flows." The Triad tool helps you to identify where you are in three different areas: your focus, language, and physiology. The diagram (see page 119) is a triangle, and each one of these areas is on one side of the triangle. Together, they create our state.

With focus, we want to know where we are putting our focus, thus our energy. If we are focused on a problem, for example, what we don't like about our neighbor, then our energy goes to that, which also affects our physiology. Let's imagine you are pissed off at your neighbor. What then happens to your body and physiological state? You might have sweaty palms, your heart rate might be elevated, your fists might be clenched, or your jaw or back might be tight. Now, think about what your language is or your inner dialogue in this situation. It might be, "What an asshole for leaving his dog poop on my lawn!" or "I can't stand that guy!" and think about when you are saying these things what it does to your focus and physiology. It probably makes you feel super negative, tight, and angry. They all work together to create the state we are living in now.

Here's the key to this. What state do you want to live in? Think of yourself in a peak state. Your peak state is how you feel, what you do with your body, and your focus when you have just accomplished a dream or accomplished something incredible. Think about what your body is doing. Are your shoulders back? Are you smiling? Do you feel relaxed and ready for anything? What is your language or dialogue? Could you be saying things like "I'm amazing" and "I'm able to accomplish anything I put my mind to"? Where is your focus? It's on the good and the possible!

At the end of this chapter, I encourage you to do the state exercise and fill in what your peak state looks like. I did this with my coach, and she even had me assign a color to my peak state, which then led me to give it a name. I call my peak state "Sunshine Fierce," and of course, my color is yellow! I associated a bright light with it because, in my peak state, I want to inspire, illuminate, and help people find their light. I added "fierce" to sunshine because I know it takes work, determination, and courage to work through hard things and be vulnerable and share. I look forward to hearing what your peak state is, and I love doing this exercise with my clients.

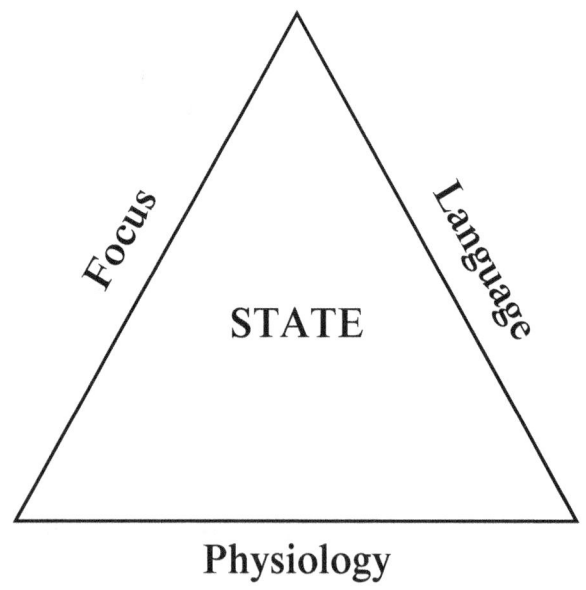

Physiology: Change your posture and gesture to match what you need to feel (think of these strong pictures warrior, lover, hero, soldier)
Focus: Creates feelings
Language: Creates meanings which create feelings

EGO: EDGING GOD OUT

I remember my mom taught me that the EGO stands for "edging God out." Even though I didn't always reach out with humility for God's assistance, I knew it was always there. It can be tempting to work only on the brain and neural pathways, the tapes that run, and think this is the work. For me, I recognized that the pain was deep, and I would need some support to heal. I realized there was a lot of anger, and underneath that was sadness, too, a lot of it. The coping mechanisms can vary after you've been bullied. Some people become survivors; some wilt like an unwatered flower and turn into a mousy version of themselves. Some achieve to be seen and feel worthy; some can't handle it at all and remove themselves from this life. These happen when we forget to humble ourselves to invite God in. The ego wants to protect. It wants to control; it wants to survive and be on top no matter what, or hide and not be criticized. As I began my healing process, I would lay aside my ego time and time again to humbly ask for God to comfort me and give me the strength to keep growing.

In one specific instance, I was struggling with someone close to me. This person was not always kind and would do things that were passive-aggressive and sometimes mean. I didn't feel their love and support, and I found myself turning into an angry person, creating more separation between us. I was surviving and protecting myself by complaining about this person and harboring bad feelings. One day, and I believe this was an angel message, a thought from God, I received a message, "Brooke, what kind of person do you want to be?"

It was a stunning thought; it was jarring. I very quickly answered, "I want to be a loving person." And so, at this moment, though it took practice and good boundaries to go with it, I chose to be a loving person. I practiced sending this person loving messages in my mind. I would even write letters to them in my journal about what I hoped for in our relationship and how I wanted to feel, and I would include, however hard, that I loved them. I would practice being loving when in their presence while practicing better boundaries when I spent time with them, and I would pray first to be a force for love before I was in their presence. I was inviting God in instead of letting my ego edge God out. The trick is to use rigorous honesty and be aware of what has happened to you. What is the difference between rigorous honesty and brutal honesty?

Rigorous honesty is a practice of being truthful with oneself and others in a thoughtful, respectful, and empathetic way. It involves being truthful about your feelings, thoughts, and behaviors and communicating them in a way that's clear, compassionate, and respectful. Rigorous honesty also involves taking responsibility for your actions, being accountable for their consequences, and setting healthy boundaries. On the other hand, brutal honesty is an approach that focuses solely on telling the truth without regard for the impact it may have on others. It involves being blunt, direct, and often insensitive in delivering feedback or opinions. Brutal honesty may come across as harsh, critical, or hurtful and can damage relationships and trust.

Take the time to process, but don't let your ego take over to try to protect you. Instead, apply healthy boundaries and invite reciprocal relationships, safe relationships where you are supported for exactly where you are and who you are trying to become.

WHAT I'VE LEARNED

Just like how a parent wants their child to feel safe and secure, the mind wants to keep us comfortable because it perceives change and growth as potential threats to our well-being. It's like a parent who is hesitant to let their child explore new territory or take risks because they fear that their child may get hurt. In the same way, our mind wants to keep us within our comfort zone because it perceives it as a safe space where we are less likely to encounter threats or difficulties. However, just like how a parent must eventually allow their child to take risks and grow to develop and thrive, we must push ourselves out of our comfort zones to learn, grow, and achieve our goals.

Even though I had become a little numb to all the hardship and challenge, this goes back to the coping mechanism of toughing it out and swallowing the tears so I didn't receive attention as a victim. After all, attention had become a destroyer of relationships and bonds for me, or at least the ones I was working to keep.

What You Can Do

You are already one step closer to becoming the person you want to be! I wish I had this information when I was younger. Now that you have a vision board, you can see more clearly who you are and who you want to become. You can write out your manifesto by writing what you want to create in every area of your life. You can assess your current state with the wheel of life (see *Action Step* in Chapter 11) and then assess it again three months down the road to make sure you are growing in each area.

When things are uncomfortable, the human instinct wants to protect you and take you back to the comfortable way of doing things. The human mind can be thought of as a protective parent who wants to shield their child from harm and discomfort. To grow, we must get uncomfortable at first. Sharing your story and letting the emotion out can be extremely vulnerable, but just remember you can get to the other side. I did, and it wasn't easy, but I was willing to work. I recommend working with a therapist and a coach if you can; as the Bible says, "Separate the wheat from the chaff." Understand what human nature does and how it comes at you, but it doesn't need to break you. Awareness of how you've taken the blows and perhaps taken them in and then asking for help to process through it is key.

Remember, separating limiting beliefs from empowering beliefs is an ongoing process. It takes time and effort to change deeply ingrained beliefs, but with persistence and a willingness to challenge yourself, you can overcome your limiting beliefs and achieve your full potential.

You CAN do this! Dr. Seuss' first children's book, *And to Think That I Saw It on Mulberry Street*, was rejected by twenty-seven publishers. The twenty-eighth publisher sold six million copies of the book. It's never all going to go exactly according to plan, but keeping this mindset will serve you beyond what you can imagine. It has for me.

REFLECTION QUESTIONS

So, how do we create this vision and the state that we want to live in? There are so many ways that we can do this, but it begins with asking yourself some key questions. Creating a mental state that we want to live with involves intentional self-awareness and ongoing personal development. To begin, it's essential to identify the mental state you aspire to maintain, such as one of calm, positivity, resilience, or contentment. Reflect on your core values and desires and consider the following questions.

1. What thoughts or beliefs contribute to the mental state you desire?
2. When you are feeling at your best, what does your body look like? Are you smiling, standing tall, shoulders back,

etc.? Take a few moments to visualize an empowered state and write what that looks like.

3. When you are feeling at your best, what thoughts go through your mind? Write them down.
4. What triggers or situations challenge this desired state?
5. What habits or practices can you incorporate to maintain it?
6. How can you react differently to stress or adversity?
7. How do your daily routines and choices influence your mental well-being?
8. What support systems or resources can you access?

ACTION STEP: CREATE YOUR PEAK STATE

Fill out the triad below with your peak state answers. Give your peak state a color, a name, affirmations, physiology, and focus, filling out each side of the triangle.

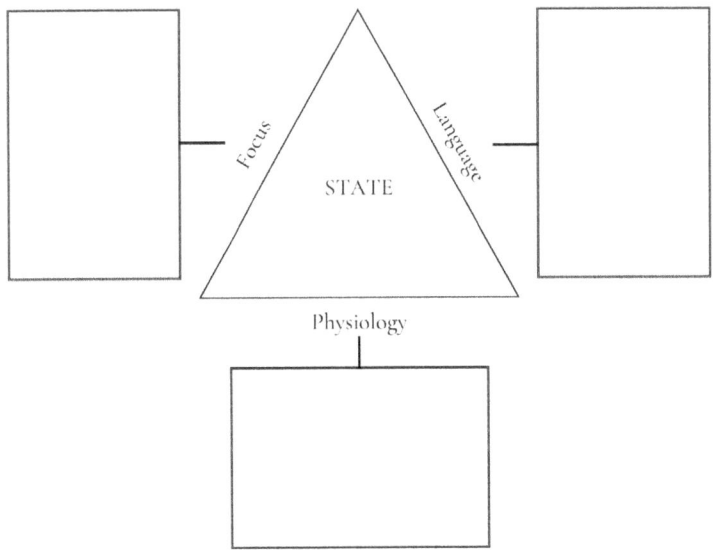

CHAPTER 8

CURATING YOUR RELATIONSHIP LIFE

Surround yourself with people who believe in your dreams, encourage your ideas, support your ambitions, and bring out the best in you.
Roy T. Bennett

Throughout my life, there has been a theme of wanting to be part of social groups and trying really hard to be accepted and liked. I'm sure some of this came from the hurtful actions of various friends or classmates over the years. This isn't something I really healed from until I realized I had zero control over other people's behavior. I had a friend challenge once where we couldn't agree on something we were doing together. We had a minor argument over the phone. I'm sure I didn't handle it perfectly, but neither did she. She chose to shut the conversation down, so there was no way to talk it out. She refused to speak to me, discuss solutions, and completely stopped communicating.

I tried and tried, out of guilt, taking it all on. I tried to call, wrote her a letter, and continued trying. She wrote me a letter saying that I didn't act with grace and provided no opportunity to resolve the issue. We stopped being friends. The loss of this friendship deeply saddened me. We had spent so many good times together over the years; our families were friends, and worst of all, I felt responsible for a long time for the friendship dissolving. I ruminated for months about what I could have done differently or how I could have fixed it.

But then, one day, I had a moment of realization while writing in my journal. I admitted I didn't want a friendship with someone who wouldn't do the work and accept that when a challenge happens, it takes two to tango! This was part of my training for finding reciprocal relationships. I also realized that I couldn't make someone like me or accept me for who I am, mistakes and all. We will all make mistakes from time to time. We are human! And it's important that we find those safe relationships where the person we are in a relationship with will know that no matter what we do to mess it up, our heart is good!

I had developed a survival mechanism of trying to control others' behavior, and I didn't even realize it. Still, I was tricked by my ego into staying in victim mode and doing a lot of angry and reactive venting about what others were doing. I spent a lot of energy feeling bad that I wasn't included in social events and other activities, and I wasted a lot of time!

I just heard Mel Robbins share a principle called "Let Them" on social media. It is so powerful! This principle basically says that if a group of girls are going out to an event together and you are not invited, let them! Let them go, and don't try to control what others are doing. As you heal and grow, the right people will come into your experience. I'm a firm believer that energy attracts energy. If you are controlling, insecure, and unsure of your values, this is the type of people you will attract.

On the other hand, if you are confident and living your values, you will attract people who share similar values. Being left out and having FOMO, the fear of missing out, has happened to me a lot over the years, and I used to agonize over it. This came from the past and the loneliness and isolation that came from being bullied and abandoned by friends.

As I did my work on it, though, I slowly learned that if people leave you out or move away from you, it's okay. I learned the hard way the "Let Them" principle. I am sharing it with you now so that you know you aren't alone if you are being left out. It's happened to me, and, as you read in the last chapter, countless others and very successful people have also gone through the same thing. Like minds gravitate together, and wouldn't you rather be with people who wanted you there? The more you try to control what others do and take the focus off your own growth, the more miserable you will be. I now "Let them." I release all friends and acquaintances to do what they do. When you release people to do what they want to do, you learn a lot about who they are and where they fit into your friend circles. You are also then free to give to those you want to be in a relationship with. I also curate my relationships very carefully. This is its own masterpiece I am creating, called my "relationship life."

Part of your vision can include an entirely separate focus on what kind of relationships you want to have in your life. Relationships require energy and investment, just as a new business or building a home or any project. They take energy. So, what kind of energy would you like to put in and get out of your relationships? Getting clear on what you want your relationship life to look like can help you navigate and attract what you want in relationships. Now that you know that when your relationship with yourself is intact and healthy, you can begin opening yourself to new connections and know how to create healthy boundaries.

LOVE IS FREEDOM

The first thing to remember is there is no such thing as perfection in humans. We are all connected as human beings, and we all make mistakes, go through challenges, find coping mechanisms, and do the best we can. Even when people act awful, it's a cry for love. Marianne Williamson says, "Everything we do is either an act of love or a cry for help." You are not, however, responsible for someone else, and it's good to take time to separate what belongs to you and what belongs to someone else. I spent many years taking on other people's issues and problems at my own expense. A great way to sort this out is to determine if the relationship you are in allows freedom of expression and the ability to be yourself. This includes not being made to feel guilty or feel bad about feeling a certain way about something. It includes someone being there for you despite your challenges and having a connection with someone who accepts you exactly as you are but challenges you to be better.

One of my favorite quotes about relationships comes from the book *Lighter* by Yung Pueblo. "Love has many synonyms, including mental clarity, compassion, selflessness, flexibility, attention, acceptance, and understanding. It is so powerful because it is simultaneously hardy and elastic, like water. Love takes on the form it needs to bind people together in a wholesome, nourishing manner. But human beings are complex, and we carry the baggage of survivalist tendencies that we gathered during the tough times. Love is freedom, while attachment is control—and all human beings enter relationships as a mix of both."[33]

Love is freedom. This is such a powerful statement. When you are in a healthy love, you feel completely free to be who you are. One of my favorite shows is *Ted Lasso*. Those of you who watch this show may understand what I am about to say. If you haven't watched it, I highly recommend it. I was moved to tears so many times by Ted's lighthearted and kind way of leading his team. He was not egotistical and always

---

33   Yung Pueblo, *Lighter: Let Go of the Past, Connect with the Present, Expand the Future* (London: Rider, an imprint of Ebury Publishing, 2022).

kind. He allowed those around him to shine and didn't feel the need to put people in their place. He had a truly unique approach to relationships that not many of us are evolved enough yet to try. I am practicing it now!

Whether it was with his players or fellow staff members on the show, even the ones who were on the opposing teams, he always responded with warmth and authenticity to every interaction. He understood the power of empathy, listening attentively to others and making them feel valued and heard. On the show, Ted builds meaningful connections, going beyond the surface level to truly understand the people he encounters. He fosters an environment of trust and support, encouraging open communication and teamwork. Ted's ability to find the best in others inspired those around him to do the same, creating a bond that extended beyond the field.

This example of how to be in relationships is a testament to the transformative power of kindness, compassion, and a genuine interest in others, leaving a lasting impact on everyone lucky enough to know him.

A Capacity for Forgiveness

My favorite example of Ted Lasso's capacity for forgiveness can be seen in his relationship with Jamie Tartt, a talented yet arrogant player on the team. Initially, Jamie's ego and diva-like behavior created a rift between him and the rest of the team, causing a toxic atmosphere within the locker room. Rather than holding a grudge or giving up on Jamie, Ted chose to approach the situation with understanding and compassion. He recognized that behind Jamie's arrogant facade was a deeply insecure individual seeking validation. Ted went out of his way to connect with Jamie on a personal level, engaging in honest conversations and offering a supportive shoulder. Instead of punishing Jamie for his past behavior, Ted forgave him and gave him a chance at redemption. This act of forgiveness allowed Jamie to let go of his defensive attitude and embrace the camaraderie within the team. Ted's ability to forgive and believe in people's capacity to change not only transformed Jamie's character, but also demonstrated the transformative power of forgiveness and compassion in building stronger relationships.

I think it's important to reiterate that there are no perfect humans or perfect relationships, but you can have a perfect container for relationships. At the risk of oversimplifying the relationship dynamic, I think Ted Lasso's approach is close to genius. Yes, it's just a TV show, but I know someone quite like Ted. I know it's possible to adopt these qualities and to use this as your connective relationship approach. What you give is usually what you receive. My dad always told me, "Giving is receiving." When I was at my worst moments with the bullying, this seemed like a cruel piece of advice. I was giving kindness, and I was receiving nothing but awfulness in return. So, let's adjust that advice just a touch. Giving, in the safe container of a kind and compassionate relationship, is receiving—at least for the ones you bring close to you.

SAFE RELATIONSHIPS

Recently, a family member was going through a challenge in a relationship with a friend. We were discussing the situation, and later, this person came back to me and shared, "You know, I don't think my friendship with this person is what I thought it was because I don't think I can tell them what I really feel about it and how their actions have affected me. Nor do I think it would make a difference." After some thought, the family member determined one of their primary criteria for a friend is whether they can tell the truth to them or not and be heard. This relationship had no transparency or ability to communicate, and upon examination, they decided to change the nature of the relationship and how it was categorized.

While working with one of my coaches, she gave me an exercise to do to categorize my friendships. This tool offered a clear picture of where my relationships stood. She had me create a center circle that she called my inner circle and asked me to describe the relationship qualities in detail for someone to make it in my inner circle (see page 131). The next circle around the inner circle was my best friends, and she asked me to write out who my best friends were and what the qualities and expectations I had for them to be called my best friends were. The next level of relationship was acquaintances. These people also had certain qualities and expectations to be placed in this category. Finally, the outer ring was called outsiders and I think we all know what that means! Those are the people that you keep your guard up with and at arm's length. Just like in the previous family member's example, they are possibly someone you can't speak openly with in a safe way.

This tool brought so much clarity for me about who I could really trust and let in and highlighted the idea that it was my choice! I had the power to choose what qualities I wanted in my inner circle, and it was okay if it was just one trusted person. I think many of us go around wearing our hearts on our sleeves and trusting far too many people with our innermost thoughts and emotions. Some of us do the opposite, and we don't let anyone in for fear of being burned and then everywhere in between. The important lesson I learned from this exercise is that there are different types of friendship, and I get to choose who I let in at each level and what that looks like. Below, you can see my example, and then in the Action Step at the end of the chapter, there is a blank one for you to fill out your own friendship circle. This can be a game-changer for your relationships!

I've had this quote posted on my wall for quite some time now:

Trust is earned, respect is given, and loyalty is demonstrated. Betrayal of any of these is to lose all three.
Ziad K. Abdelnour

You and only you can determine who gets access to your inner circle and gets to be called a best friend. Take this to heart and take the time to decide what qualities you will let into your emotional home. Think of your relationship categories as you would when considering who you would let into certain rooms of your home. Would you let an acquaintance come into your bedroom? They would likely be invited into the living room, and those who have a big presence in your life might be invited to hang out in the kitchen. Are they supportive? Do they see the best in you and show and communicate love to you? Will they take time to hear you and sort out your differences in a respectful way? Is there anyone in your home who is tracking in dirt and making life difficult for you and should not be in your life? You get to choose!

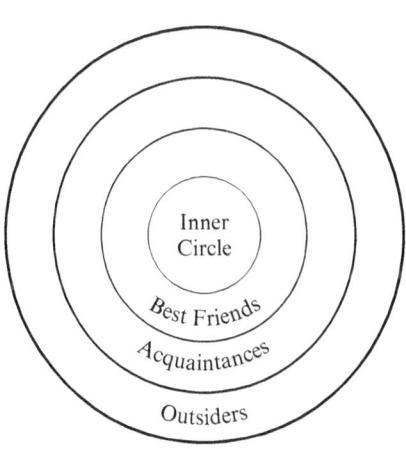

In a safe relationship, both partners respect each other's boundaries, opinions, and individuality. They value each other's feelings, needs, and perspectives. There is no belittling, insulting, or demeaning behavior. Regular communication is essential for a safe relationship. Both partners feel comfortable expressing their thoughts, concerns, and emotions openly and honestly. They actively listen to each other, validate each other's feelings, and work together to resolve conflicts or disagreements in a constructive manner.

Emotional Safety

When I first met Derek, I had brought some baggage with me. I was working on setting it down and moving on, but it was still there being processed, and I was trying to grow. He provided a safe space for me to share and never judged me. He saw my regret about some of my decisions and loved me anyway. He did not do the work for me, but helped me feel safe enough to dig into my own shame, guilt, and heaviness I felt. He saw the good in me. I felt like I couldn't screw it up! In a safe relationship, both partners feel like this! They can share their vulnerabilities without fear of ridicule or rejection.

There is support, empathy, and understanding from both sides. Emotional safety allows individuals to be their authentic selves, and it fosters intimacy and connection. There is equality and mutual respect. The next one is key! Power and decision-making are shared, and both partners have an equal voice in the relationship. There is no dominance or control exerted by one partner over the other. Boy, do I know about this one! It's easy to see after you've gone through something, but if you are feeling controlled or dominated, it's time to step up and work on yourself so you can ask for what you need and determine if this relationship is healthy for you.

Physical Safety

Physical safety is a fundamental aspect of a safe relationship. There is no physical abuse, violence, or intimidation. Both partners feel safe and secure in each other's presence.

After I found out I was pregnant with my daughter, and it became clear the relationship with her father was not a healthy one, I felt alone. I had friends, but many were from my past. They didn't know how to adjust to me being one of the first to have a child, and my current relationship had isolated me from many of my friends. I had to really spend a lot of time alone figuring things out. At the time, it felt awful. I mean, my life had been turned upside down, and I was scared. It was then that I reached out to God and asked for guidance. It was one of those "show me the way" moments where I didn't feel amazing, and my confidence had been shaken.

Things weren't as I envisioned them to be. I felt that God took me by the hand and showed me that taking care of the basics and myself little by little could build back my confidence. I began paying off my bills and organizing my apartment, preparing the way for my daughter. I began reading my Bible again, spending time doing things I enjoyed, and sticking close to the support of my family. I truly appreciated the one friend who had stuck with me all along, and she was there for me during this challenging time.

Remember that a safe relationship requires ongoing effort, commitment, and communication from both partners. It is a dynamic process that evolves over time. If you have concerns about the safety of your relationship, it is important to seek support from trusted friends, family, or professionals who can provide guidance and assistance.

If you need additional support in an abusive relationship, see Appendix B at the back of this book.

BUILD NEW FRIENDSHIPS

The Bible encourages us to be in community and fellowship. While solitude can have its benefits, the Bible also emphasizes the importance of community and fellowship. Hebrews 10:24–25 encourages us to "consider how to stir up one another to love and good works, not neglecting to meet together, as is the habit of some, but encouraging one another."

If you find yourself in a situation where you don't have any friends, it can be challenging, but there are steps you can take to improve your social connections and build new friendships. You can spend some time reflecting on yourself: your interests, hobbies, and values. Knowing yourself better can help you connect with like-minded individuals. Pursue your interests by engaging in activities and hobbies that genuinely interest you. Join clubs, classes, or groups related to your interests. This provides an opportunity to meet people with similar passions and increases your chances of making friends.

Remember to be open and approachable. It's even a good idea to practice being open and friendly in your interactions. Smile, make eye contact, and show genuine interest in others. Be approachable and initiate conversations when you find common ground with someone. I've often given my daughters this advice when they feel lonely: Consider volunteering for a cause or organization that aligns with your values. Volunteering not only allows you to give back to the community, but also offers opportunities to meet new people who share your interests—going to social events and gatherings like local events, meetups, or social gatherings in your community. Attend them with an open mind, and don't be afraid to strike up conversations with people. Remember, many others may also be looking to make new friends, and most of the time, people aren't thinking about you; they are dealing with their own social anxiety.

I'm not as big of a fan of this idea, but it can work for you if you're a little more introverted. Try to join online communities, forums, or social media groups focused on your interests. Engage in conversations, ask questions, and contribute meaningfully. This can lead to virtual friendships and potentially offline connections.

WHAT I'VE LEARNED

True friends are those rare people who come to find you
in dark places and lead you back to the light.
Steven Aitchison

It's okay to ask for support, have boundaries, and require the ones you bring in close to treat you with kindness and respect. It only takes one supporter to make a difference in your life, someone who believes in your dreams and supports and encourages you. My grandmother always said, "If you can find one true friend, you've found gold."

A safe relationship is characterized by mutual trust, respect, and emotional security. It is a relationship in which both partners feel comfortable being themselves and expressing their thoughts and feelings without fear of judgment or harm. Trust is the foundation of a safe relationship. Both partners trust each other's words, actions, and intentions. There is no need for constant suspicion or doubt. Trust is built through consistent honesty, reliability, and transparency.

Healthy boundaries are established and respected in a safe relationship. Each partner understands and respects the other's need for personal space, time, and autonomy. Boundaries are communicated and honored to maintain a sense of safety and personal well-being.

What You Can Do

When you have safe relationships, and you've spent time working on yourself, you can do anything you put your mind to. Be selective. Curate your relationship life with intention. Know the qualities you are looking for and the kind of people that you want in your life. Only let the ones in close that will tell you the truth. You can speak your truth and be heard, and it's so important to be able to have someone who loves you at your best and your worst if there is mutual respect for one another's feelings.

Focus on your physical and mental well-being, pursue your passions, and build a fulfilling life for yourself. Remember to be patient and know that building genuine friendships takes time, so be patient and persistent. It may take several attempts or encounters before you find people with whom you genuinely connect. Don't get discouraged by setbacks, and keep putting yourself out there. Making friends is a two-way process. It requires effort, empathy, and mutual investment. As you work on building new friendships, be sure to be a good friend yourself by being supportive, trustworthy, and understanding, and do it in the safe container of a kind and compassionate friend. If you aren't sure yet about someone, let them show you by slowly getting to know them, and believe them when they show you! Their actions will always speak louder than words. If you don't understand what an action means, ask for clarification.

Most of all, take care of yourself and prioritize self-care and personal growth. When you feel good about yourself and exude confidence, it becomes easier to connect with others.

Reflection Questions

Healthy relationships are the cornerstone of a fulfilling and well-balanced life. They provide us with love, support, and a sense of belonging, helping us navigate the complexities of existence. Finding and maintaining healthy relationships, whether they are romantic, platonic, or familial, is a vital aspect of personal growth and well-being. To embark on this journey, it is crucial to start with self-reflection and ask the right questions.

Here are some reflection questions to guide you in finding and nurturing healthy relationships. As you reflect on these questions, you'll gain a deeper understanding of your own desires and boundaries, and you'll be better equipped to form and maintain healthy, meaningful relationships that contribute positively to your life.

1. Does your friend or partner:
    a. evaluate, judge, or belittle?
    b. try to fix you or the situation?
    c. try to make it about themselves, their past losses, and how they grieve?
    d. accept you as you are?
    e. know the greatest gift they can give is their presence?
    f. listen to your heart, not just your words?
2. What are your core values and beliefs about relationships, and how do they influence your choices in partners and friends?
3. Are you in a healthy relationship with yourself? How do you treat and care for your own well-being?
4. What qualities and values are non-negotiable in your relationships, and where are you willing to compromise?
5. Reflect on your past relationships, both positive and negative. What have you learned from them, and how have they shaped your expectations?
6. How do you communicate with others, and are you an active listener? Are there areas where you can improve your communication skills?

7. What boundaries do you need to establish and maintain in your relationships to ensure your emotional and physical well-being?
8. Are you seeking relationships out of loneliness or necessity, or are you genuinely connecting with others based on shared values and mutual respect?
9. Consider the people in your life currently. Do they uplift and support you, or do they bring negativity and stress? What changes might be necessary?
10. What role does forgiveness play in your relationships, and how do you handle conflicts and disagreements?
11. How do you envision a healthy and fulfilling relationship? What steps can you take to move closer to that ideal?

ACTION STEP: CREATE YOUR RELATIONSHIP CIRCLES

Embracing the wisdom of Tony Robbins has been transformative in many aspects of my life, particularly through his insightful teaching on the "Friendship Circles" diagram. This powerful visual representation outlines concentric circles, each delineating a layer of our social connections: the inner circle, best friends, acquaintances, and outsiders. Robbins encourages us to deliberate thoughtfully on who enters these circles and to establish the values that guide these decisions. As a coach, mom, wife, and friend, this concept has been a guiding light, shaping the way I navigate relationships and allocate my emotional energy. Join me on a journey into the profound impact of Friendship Circles and how its principles have enriched my roles and relationships, offering valuable insights into the dynamics of connection and the importance of intentional choices in fostering a fulfilling and meaningful life.

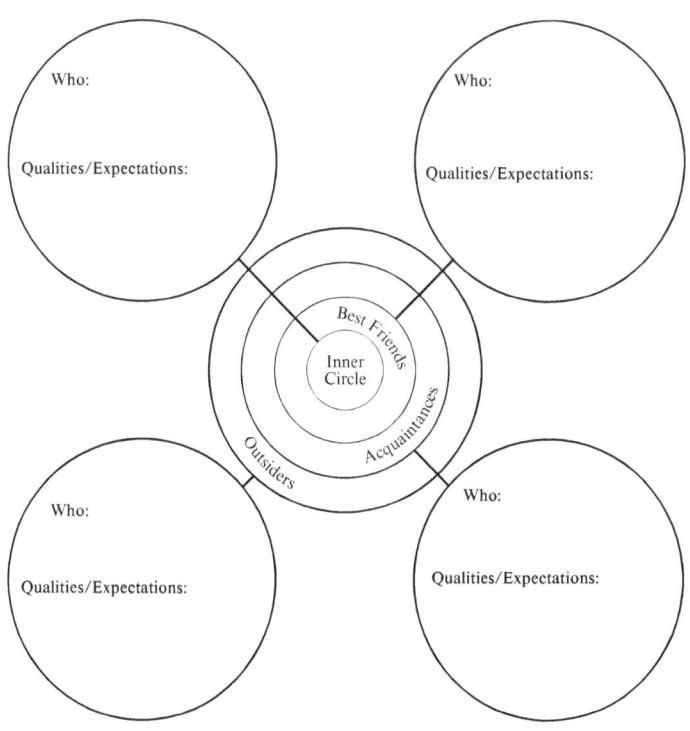

Who:

Qualities/Expectations:

Who:

Qualities/Expectations:

Best Friends

Inner Circle

Acquaintances

Outsiders

Who:

Qualities/Expectations:

Who:

Qualities/Expectations:

CHAPTER 9

KEEP THE FAITH

*A real friend is one who walks in when the rest of the
world walks out.*
Walter Winchell

When I moved back to Oregon and was pregnant with Paige, realizing that I was not going to continue living with her biological dad, I felt so alone. I was slipping into depression and found it hard to get out of bed. I also had morning sickness and struggled to feel physically well for at least the first four months. I felt very alone. I was alone with my decisions and my sadness about failed relationships; my high school friends had moved on, and my college friends were moving on to build their lives and their careers. I had just moved 3000 miles back to my hometown in Oregon from Florida.

I knew that Sam's family didn't like me and especially didn't like that I took him away from their family life in Florida. I felt trapped by the heavy burden of responsibility, and I felt my dreams slipping away. It was getting harder and harder to be optimistic and look towards the light. My body was changing, and I anticipated being a single mom. I had one thing to turn to, and that was my faith. I remember actually standing in the shower one day and letting out a really good cry and actually going through the physical act of getting on my knees, and I pleaded with God, "Show me the way!"

My prayers haven't always been very sophisticated, but this one packed a big punch. I could feel that something had changed in me. There was a deep sense of humility and trust, giving my full trust over to God and releasing my story to Him. It was at this point things began to change in how I felt.

The Bible does not specifically address the concept of being alone in every context. However, it does provide guidance and principles that can be applied to various situations, including times when you are alone. There were times on my healing journey when I felt very alone, and I found it comforting and helpful to reach out to the Bible. The Bible assures us that, even when you are alone, you are never truly alone because God is with you. Hebrews 13:5 says, "Keep your lives free from the love of money and be content with what you have, because God has said, 'Never will I leave you; never will I forsake you.'" The Bible encourages individuals to use times of solitude to seek God and draw closer to Him.

In Matthew 6:6, Jesus advises His followers, "But when you pray, go into your room, close the door, and pray to your Father, who is unseen. Then your Father, who sees what is done in secret, will reward you." The Bible encourages introspection and self-examination, which can be done in times of solitude. Psalm 25:16 says, "Turn to me and be gracious to me, for I am lonely and afflicted."

When Jesus was alone and being tempted by the devil, it was a significant event in His life that highlighted His strength of character and unwavering commitment to His divine purpose. The story of Jesus' temptation can be found in the New Testament of the Bible, specifically in the books of Matthew (4:1–11), Mark (1:12–13), and Luke (4:1–13).

In this chapter of my book, I share a deeply personal journey where the teachings of the Bible became a source of solace and healing in the aftermath of emotional trauma. While I recognize that not everyone may share my belief in the Bible, the intention of this chapter is not to prescribe a particular faith but rather to offer a perspective on the broader theme of spiritual healing. Regardless of religious affiliations, the message resonates with the idea that individuals can find strength and resilience through their own spiritual means. This chapter serves as an invitation for you to explore your own spiritual resources, whatever they may be, as a pathway toward healing from emotional wounds. It's a testament to the diverse ways in which we can draw on our inner reserves to navigate the challenges of life and emerge whole again.

Draw Closer to the Lord in Times of Distress

Lamentations 3:40 says, "Let us examine our ways and test them, and let us return to the Lord." During times of loneliness or distress, the Bible teaches that God is a source of comfort and companionship. Once, when I was in high school, I went climbing in the Colorado mountains with a group from my summer camp. We had set out early to climb one of the collegiate peaks with our forty-pound packs and all our food and supplies to make it for a climb and an overnight stay in the mountains. We climbed all morning and peaked Mt. Harvard before 1 p.m. Some of us felt ambitious and wanted to keep going, so part of the group returned to the base camp, and a few of us pressed on to Colombia Peak. It was a challenge, and as the climb over the ridge between the two mountains progressed, I felt blisters developing on my feet. I was wearing my mom's old hiking boots she used while trekking through Europe when she was young and dating my dad.

These weren't the kind of boots you find at REI these days! Nice and firm and not really broken into for my feet. There's a rule that when climbing in Colorado, you want to peak before 1 or 2 p.m. as the weather can turn at that altitude quickly. Sure enough, as we stumbled through the loose rock toward the top of the second peak, the snow fell, and the weather changed. I was definitely feeling more and more fatigued and needed rest breaks. My feet were burning, and the blisters were getting worse. Mentally, I could feel myself slipping a bit, too. I kept looking up ahead and seeing more to do and more work and thinking more and more about how tired and hungry I was getting, watching the snowfall and worrying, realizing that I was wearing shorts and light layers. The guide who was with us was experienced and mentally tough, very fit, and doing much better than I was. I was reaching the point where I needed a lot of encouragement even to believe I could do it because what I really wanted to do was sit and rest. Instead, he encouraged us, and we pressed on.

We finally made it to the top, and it was beautiful. I had a tremendous feeling of accomplishment, but after a brief stay at the summit, we had to think about getting back down and finding our base camp where the others were. I was so hungry, and my feet were raw inside the boots. It was later than we wanted to get up there because of the stops and rests we required. It started getting dark, and I remember reaching out to God and asking for the strength to keep going so that I could make it back to camp. The darkness descended upon us quickly, and the rocks were unstable under my feet. I felt like crying. I began to feel afraid because I could see our guide was getting concerned about finding the camp.

They had a call they could do to signal to the group at the camp that we were trying to find them. The idea was you would call it out, and then the group would call back to you, and we would follow their voice. We didn't have anything to stay the night out in the wilderness; it was dark and getting colder. All our belongings were at base camp, and we had finished our snacks and water. Floyd called out to our group, and all that answered was the silence of the wilderness and the sounds of the animals and bugs. I clung to my mom's shared wisdom that I was never alone and that I could reach out to God at any time.

I just quietly asked God to bring us safely home to our group, even though I couldn't humanly imagine how we would find them coming off a mountain in the middle of nowhere in the dark without even a clear trail to follow. I knew our guide had faith and was praying, too, so I trusted that we would find our way and shut out any fearful thoughts. Eventually, off in the distance, we could hear a return to our calls, and we were able to follow their voices to camp. I had a very clear feeling that God had guided us to them and them to hear us. Having gone through this experience gave me confidence that no matter what mountain or hurdle I would encounter in life, God would be there to give me the strength to proceed and find my way.

I have had many experiences like this. One other was when I had gotten caught in a snowstorm in Bend, Oregon, and suddenly lost control of my car. At the time, I didn't know how to control a car that was fishtailing, which is embarrassing to admit since my husband is a race car driver! This was before Skip Barber Racing School, and I had no training on how to control a car. I slid out of control into the oncoming traffic lane. I had zero control of the car and no idea what to do, so I cried out to God. I said, "God help!" That was all that came out of my mouth, but it was a sincere cry for help. Alone in the car, heading toward a semi-truck in oncoming traffic, I asked God for help. And somehow, the car did a 360 turn without hitting anything and ended up backward on the opposite side of the road in a snowbank. The impact was not bad, and I was totally okay. No other vehicles were affected, and I was able to walk back for help from where I landed.

This is another clear example of God's presence and protection being made known in potentially life-threatening situations. Talking to God doesn't need to be fancy, and, while I recommend reading the Bible and familiarizing yourself with Bible stories, you don't need to have read all of it to reach out for help. I was taught that God is as close as the air you breathe and, multiple times in my life, this presence has been demonstrated by experience. You can begin now. It's never too late to reach out to God for His presence in your life.

LET SCRIPTURE BE YOUR GUIDE

The world and people will challenge you. If you've been in destructive relationships and dealt with low self-esteem as a result, you will be tempted to go backward with your standards. Attachments to people and our old ways of doing things can sometimes turn into a stronghold. A stronghold is a place of security or survival.

One of my favorite stories that teaches the strength of reliance on God to resist temptation is when Jesus was tempted by the devil. The devil tried three separate times to trick Jesus into making other material things more important than following God's direction. Each time, Jesus resisted. You can, too, with God's help! Again, all it takes is to reach out to God for guidance to lead you to healthier ways.

According to the biblical accounts, after His baptism by John the Baptist, Jesus was led by the Spirit into the wilderness. There, He fasted for forty days and nights, during which time He was tempted by the devil. The devil appeared to Jesus and presented Him with three distinct temptations, each aimed at testing His allegiance and resolve.

The first temptation challenged Jesus' physical hunger after His long period of fasting. The devil suggested that Jesus turn stones into bread to satisfy His hunger. However, Jesus responded by quoting Scripture, saying, "Man shall not live by bread alone, but by every word that proceeds out of the mouth of God." This demonstrated His reliance on God's word and His refusal to prioritize His own physical desires over spiritual nourishment.

In the second temptation, the devil took Jesus to the pinnacle of the temple and encouraged Him to jump, quoting Scripture himself, trying to test Jesus' trust in God's protection. Jesus again responded with Scripture, saying, "You shall not put the Lord your God to the test." He firmly acknowledged that it was not appropriate to test God's faithfulness by deliberately putting oneself in danger.

The third and final temptation was the most enticing. The devil brought Jesus to a high mountain and offered Him all the kingdoms of the world if He would bow down and worship him. In response, Jesus declared, "Get behind me, Satan! For it is written, 'You shall worship the Lord your God and him only shall you serve.'" Jesus recognized that His allegiance was to God alone and that He would not compromise His worship or serve any other authority.

Throughout Jesus' temptations, He consistently relied on Scripture to counter the devil. He showed a deep understanding and commitment to God's word, using it as a source of strength and guidance. By doing so, Jesus exemplified the importance of spiritual discernment and the power of relying on God's truth to resist temptation.

In each instance, Jesus triumphed over temptation by remaining steadfast in His faith and unwavering in His commitment to God's will. He set an example for humanity, showing that even in the face of intense temptation and distress, it is possible to remain faithful and obedient to God.

I found Christianity, with its foundational principles of love, forgiveness, and redemption, provides a profound framework for seeking healing from trauma. The teachings of Jesus Christ emphasize the transformative power of forgiveness and have encouraged me to let go of resentment and find peace through the act of forgiving those who hurt me. Additionally, the Christian faith offered a sense of divine love and purpose, providing assurance that I was not alone in my struggle. The promise of redemption and the belief in a higher power's unconditional love can bring you comfort and strength, serving as a beacon of hope in the process of healing from emotional wounds.

Beyond Christianity, various spiritual teachings offer unique perspectives and practices that can be equally instrumental in the healing journey. For example, Eastern philosophies like Buddhism emphasize mindfulness, meditation, and acceptance of impermanence. By cultivating awareness and letting go of attachments, individuals can find solace and resilience. Similarly, the teachings of compassion in Hinduism, the principles of balance in Taoism, or the interconnectedness in indigenous spiritualities all provide valuable insights that can guide individuals toward healing and wholeness. The common thread across these teachings lies in their ability to offer guidance, support, and a sense of purpose to those on the path of recovery from trauma, illustrating the universality of spiritual wisdom in fostering resilience and renewal. Knowing that there is a higher source of wisdom available to us can be very helpful on our healing journey. It was for me!

WHAT I'VE LEARNED

When I was a kid, my mom would always tell me, "You are never alone; God is always with you." Even though this feeling of connection with our Creator can ebb and flow, sometimes we feel the connection, and sometimes we don't as much. It was helpful to hear my mom's voice reminding me I'm never alone. It helps to have had experiences that have backed this up, where I got to know that, undeniably, there was a higher power looking out for me.

In times of challenge, and when I feel the most alone, I've always turned to God and the Bible and the stories of how Jesus overcame hardship. I often refer to the story of Jesus, alone in the wilderness, being tempted by the devil, and He overcame this temptation. So far, I have been successful at finding a relevant teaching or story in the Bible for every challenge I've faced in life.

The story of Jesus' temptation serves as a reminder of the strength we can find in our own faith when confronted with challenges and temptations. It encourages believers to seek guidance from Scripture and to rely on God's Word as a source of wisdom and strength. Jesus' victory over temptation demonstrates His divine nature and unwavering commitment to fulfilling His mission as the Son of God.

WHAT YOU CAN DO

Hopefully, these examples from Jesus's life, quotes from the Bible assuring us of God's presence, how we can use our time alone to grow spiritually, and my examples of God's protection and presence when I felt very alone and afraid, can provide you with reasons to believe that you are never alone. You always have God, even if you are feeling abandoned by friends and family. The opportunity we have when we find ourselves alone is to dig a little deeper and reflect on what kind of relationships we want in our experience and the energy and qualities we are looking to bring into our lives.

A podcaster named Charlie Ward once said, "God gave you a pair of knees, so get down on those knees and ask God!"

I loved this simple idea that if we can humble ourselves and get quiet enough to just ask God, we will get answers.

Maybe if you are alone, God is doing you a favor, closing a door so that another can be presented, taking you down a better path toward the life you were created to live. I do believe everything happens for a reason, even if we don't fully understand what that reason is. If you keep moving forward one step at a time, you will get the answers you need.

REFLECTION QUESTIONS

Drawing inspiration from the example of Jesus and inviting the presence of God into our lives can be a transformative journey that leads to a deeper sense of purpose, peace, and fulfillment. Jesus's teachings and actions emphasize love, compassion, forgiveness, and selflessness, which offer a profound guide for living a better life. By integrating these principles into our daily existence and fostering a close relationship with God, we can experience spiritual and personal growth.

Here, we explore some reflection questions to help you begin this transformative path toward a richer, more meaningful life. As you reflect on these questions, you may find new insights and a deeper sense of spiritual connection, which can guide you on the path to a more fulfilling and purpose-driven life, mirroring the principles and teachings of Jesus Christ.

1. How does Jesus's life and teachings inspire you to lead a more loving and compassionate life?
2. In what ways can you actively practice forgiveness in your daily interactions and relationships, as Jesus did?
3. Consider your daily actions and decisions. Are they aligned with the values and principles that Jesus taught?

4. What steps can you take to cultivate a deeper, more intimate relationship with God, and how might this influence your daily life?

5. Reflect on moments when you have felt God's presence in your life. What can you learn from these experiences?

6. In challenging times, how can your faith and trust in God help you navigate difficulties and find hope and strength?

7. What is your understanding of purpose and how it relates to your faith in God and your pursuit of a better life?

8. How can you extend kindness and service to others in your community, following Jesus's example of selflessness?

9. Consider the role of prayer and meditation in your life. How can these practices help you connect with God and find inner peace?

10. What are the specific areas of your life where you feel that inviting God's presence and following Jesus's example could lead to positive transformation?

ACTION STEP: SET A TIME FOR QUIET DAILY REFLECTION

One powerful action step to get closer to God is to prioritize daily prayer and meditation. Dedicate a specific time each day to connect with God through prayer and reflection. Use this time to express gratitude, seek guidance, and open your heart to the Divine presence. By establishing a consistent practice of prayer and meditation, you can foster a deeper and more meaningful relationship with God, allowing for a closer connection and a greater sense of spiritual fulfillment.

CHAPTER 10

FINDING YOUR PURPOSE AND YOUR WHY

Twenty years from now, you will be more disappointed
by the things you didn't do than by the ones you did.
So, throw off the bowlines. Sail away from the safe
harbor. Catch the trade winds in your sails. Explore.
Dream. Discover.
Mark Twain

When I married Derek, I could not have known this choice would affect my life in ways I didn't even think about. When you are finally in the right relationship with mutual respect, love, and someone who truly sees you for who you are, it allows you to bloom. This was a slow process for me, as I had to get out of my own way and sort through all the challenging relationships in my life and the aftermath. What the safety of this relationship has given me is the time and confidence to find my *why*, my reason for what I do.

Recently, I worked with a client who asked me to help her discover her purpose. She shared with me that she felt an emptiness and lack of drive in what she was currently doing and didn't know how to discover her true purpose.

As we worked together, I asked her questions about her life and her family. I asked her to tell me about her family, her childhood, and her current life with her husband. Through some time and the safety of the confidential coach and client relationship, she began to open up about some very sad times in her childhood and living with a mother who was an alcoholic and a father who cheated on her mother. She lived through divorce and felt deep sadness for losing normal childhood experiences and watching her mother go through such a hurtful and difficult time.

As we processed through it all, it came out that she loved to dance and was never able to take dance classes due to the tumultuous nature of her childhood. She expressed that she loved how dancing made her feel, and she'd never had an opportunity to do it. We talked about how she could sign up for a dance class and get out there and try it. It's never too late! It's important to peel back the layers of dysfunction and toxic relationships and understand what is at work. We can then create our relationship boundaries and understand our worth. Then, we can focus on the things that make our heart feel happy and bring us joy.

I have always dreamed of writing a book, but when it came down to it, I allowed my fears to always get in the way. When I took the leap to write my first book, a children's book, I resisted writing the outline even after I committed to the publisher. As a matter of fact, it was my husband who finally sat down with me with a pen and paper and said, "We are doing this!"

I think for many of us, it's easy to dream and think of what we could be, and it's easy to compare our lives to others and think how happy we would be if we had that life or did that thing. Still, when it comes down to it, we resist digging in and really doing the work of learning what is holding us back and what we need to do to get there. Humans are generally not very good at being uncomfortable and not trained to focus on our why. Why we are doing something is what will get us through the discomfort of doing what we need to do to become successful and move to the next level in life. Being uncomfortable is a good thing; taking risks is imperative for growth.

I found my why by following what really made my heart sing, focusing on what really made me feel a sense of deep purpose. I spent time trying and exploring things, followed the experiences that brought great joy, and worked on creating more of them. As I've shared with you, I did work to understand myself better and what my values were, and then began incorporating them into my daily life and relationships. I have been able to take the scars and turn them into stars by sharing with my clients, through my writing, and what I communicate as a life coach that we can all go through hard things and then share our story to help others avoid some of our own missteps. My why has become helping to make the world a happier place by inspiring others to work through challenges to live their dream life.

This chapter is where we really dig into what your dream is with your why attached to it so you can create your action plan in the next chapter and have the push you need to see it through.

FINDING YOUR WHY

Simon Sinek teaches about the concept of knowing your why, and coaches and growth experts use it to help entrepreneurs dig deep and take steps to become who they want to be. In a short video on YouTube, he shares a fun way to find your why.[34] Ask several of your close friends why they are friends with you. He suggests that they will likely all have a similar answer, and it will lead you to your why. He also says that

---

34 "Find Your Why | Simon Sinek," YouTube, October 6, 2021, https://www. youtube.com/watch?v=tF7YLGpOoz8.

maybe they won't know exactly at first, and they'll start saying things, and then at some point, they'll say something, and you'll respond with an emotional response like goosebumps or tears welling up. This, he suggests, is your why.

Once you do this exercise, we will begin honing in on your passion if you don't yet know exactly what it is. A great way to connect with it is to find several mentors. At the end of this chapter, there will be a helpful set of questions for you to determine this.

Your Passion Is Your Purpose

I was quickly able to define my mentors and put them into a visual document I have hanging on the wall. I look at it every day. I spent some time writing about the qualities and things I liked about these people, and then I asked myself what similar qualities I have. They all shared abilities that were similar to mine or what I wanted to create. This helped me see that I, too, could do something great. Of course, I encourage everyone to be their own unique expression of themselves.

I love this quote by Bishop T.D. Jakes: "If you can't figure out your purpose, figure out your passion. For your passion will lead you right into your purpose." I have always cared about others' happiness and inspiring people to be their best. I have also always been very determined and inspired by stories of overcoming. I love nonfiction stories of people who have overcome something or been successful. If you are still struggling to find your purpose, you might consider what you've overcome or gone through that was really challenging and how you can help others avoid this pain or struggle. Sometimes, our challenges are our greatest teachers and gifts if we let them be. God may be putting you through something to help you fulfill your purpose in helping someone.

As we identify what matters most, we can incorporate the values exploration we did earlier to get closer to our purpose. Identifying a purpose often involves aligning your personal values with the desire to make a difference in the world around you.

INSPIRING MENTORS WHO FOLLOWED THEIR PASSION

Finding mentors does not mean we copy or do exactly what someone has done, but it can point us on the path to finding our purpose. Surrounding yourself with inspiring stories, books, mentors, or role models who have found their purpose can help us learn from their journeys and experiences. Their stories can provide insights and inspiration that may spark ideas about your own purpose.

Dwayne Johnson

One celebrity who has demonstrated a strong sense of identifying their goals and achieving them is Dwayne "The Rock" Johnson. Johnson started his career as a professional wrestler in the WWE (formerly WWF) and became one of the most popular and successful wrestlers of all time. However, he didn't stop there. Johnson had a clear vision of transitioning into the world of acting and becoming a Hollywood star. Despite initial skepticism from the industry, he persisted and made his debut in the film *The Mummy Returns* in 2001. From there, he worked hard to establish himself as a leading action star. He has since appeared in numerous successful films, including *The Fast and Furious* franchise, *Jumanji: Welcome to the Jungle,* and *Moana*, where he showcased his voice acting talents.

Johnson's success as an actor didn't come easily, as he faced several setbacks along the way. But his determination, work ethic, and relentless pursuit of his goals helped him overcome obstacles. He consistently sought out diverse roles, showcasing his versatility as an actor in both action-packed films and comedies. Additionally, he leveraged his massive social media following to engage with fans and promote his projects, further solidifying his brand. Furthermore, Johnson expanded his entrepreneurial endeavors by launching his own production company, Seven Bucks Productions, which has produced successful films and television shows. He also ventured into the fitness industry, launching a line of sportswear and his own tequila brand, Teremana.

What sets Johnson apart is his ability to adapt and reinvent himself while staying true to his values and work ethic. He recognized where he wanted to be, set clear goals, and consistently worked toward them. Johnson's charisma, determination, and talent have helped him become one of the highest-paid and most recognizable celebrities in the world. His success story serves as an inspiration for those who strive to identify their goals and work tirelessly to achieve them.

Princess Diana

Princess Diana, born Diana Frances Spencer, achieved immense success and left a lasting impact as a prominent figure in the British royal family. While her life tragically ended prematurely, her legacy continues to inspire and captivate people around the world. Diana's path to success began when she married Prince Charles in 1981, becoming the Princess of Wales. From the moment she stepped into the royal spotlight, Diana captivated the public's attention with her charisma, grace, and compassion. She quickly became one of the most beloved members of the royal family.

One of the key reasons for Diana's success was her genuine empathy and her ability to connect with people from all walks of life. She used her platform to draw attention to charitable causes and bring awareness to important issues such as homelessness, HIV/AIDS, landmines, and mental health. Diana's hands-on approach to philanthropy broke down barriers and challenged the traditional role of the royal family. Her iconic involvement with HIV/AIDS organizations helped reduce the stigma surrounding the disease, and she played a pivotal role in changing public perception and encouraging empathy and compassion. Additionally, Diana's commitment to landmine awareness resulted in a global ban on anti-personnel landmines, making a significant impact on human rights and international disarmament efforts.

Diana's success also lay in her ability to connect with people on a personal level. Her warmth and approachability made her relatable, and she used her platform to highlight the struggles and challenges faced by those marginalized in society. Her empathy resonated deeply with people, and she became known as the "People's Princess." Moreover, Diana's fashion choices and sense of style also played a significant role in her success. Her fashion choices were closely followed and emulated by people worldwide, establishing her as a style icon. She used her influence to promote British fashion designers and brought a fresh and modern approach to royal fashion.

Despite her untimely death in 1997, Princess Diana's legacy lives on. Her humanitarian work, her commitment to compassion, and her genuine concern for others continue to inspire people to this day. Diana's success can be attributed to her authenticity, her passion for making a difference, and her unwavering dedication to using her position to bring positive change to the world.

FINDING YOUR PURPOSE WITH IKIGAI

"Ikigai," a Japanese concept that roughly translates to "a reason for being," is a powerful tool for finding your purpose in life. It encourages individuals to seek the intersection of four fundamental elements: what you love, what you're good at, what the world needs, and what you can be paid for. By identifying where these aspects overlap, you can uncover your ikigai and discover a deeper sense of purpose.

When you do what you love, excel at it, contribute to a meaningful cause, and find financial reward, you're likely to experience a profound sense of fulfillment and contentment. It's a process of self-discovery that involves introspection and reflection on your passions, strengths, values, and the needs of your community or the world. Ikigai serves as a guiding principle for living a purposeful life and helps you align your actions and goals with your innermost desires and the greater good. It's a reminder that our purpose often lies at the intersection of personal happiness and societal significance.

Remember that finding your purpose is a deeply personal journey, and it may evolve and change over time. Be patient with yourself, trust the process, and listen to your inner voice. Ikigai encourages a holistic approach, integrating mind, body, and spirit to help you live authentically and align with your purpose. The concept of ikigai as a purpose in life with both personal and social dimensions is captured by the well-known ikigai diagram. This diagram includes overlapping spheres covering:

- What you love.
- What you are good at.
- What the world needs.
- What you can get paid for.

What do you LOVE?

Passion   Mission

What are you   ikigai   What the world
good at?   needs.

Profession   Vocation

What you can
be paid for.

What I've Learned

I wholeheartedly believe that we know ourselves better than anyone else, but we spend a lifetime learning to be nice, follow the rules, get along, and do as we are told. Slowly, our best gifts and our purpose get muddled with junk, some of it well-intentioned junk, that those who love us teach us either by their unconscious habits or programming or beliefs. The good news is that we are also taught good things. You don't have to divorce your extended family or pay your parents a visit and holler at them for what they taught you. Most of the time, our parents teach us things they think will help us get along better in life, and the intention is good. However, sometimes their baggage is so heavy that they teach you things that are not healthy.

What You Can Do

Believe it or not, you already have a profound impact on the lives of some of the people who are closest to you—you just must ask! And you already know your innermost being, who you are. It is your responsibility to separate the wheat from the tares (weeds) and decide what will be helpful, positive, and keep you moving toward who you want to be. It is your job to define exactly who you want to be and how you want to show up and to reach out for help and tools to become that person.

Now that you are getting closer to your purpose, it's important to remember to stay focused on what you want to become now. You have done a lot of processing of the past and what you've been through, and this will continue throughout your lifetime. Hopefully, you incorporate this into your daily activity by journaling your thoughts and feelings so you can stay aware of what will come up from the past from time to time.

- **Identify Core Values:** Your core values are the guiding principles that underpin your actions and decisions. Write a list of your core values and prioritize them. Consider values like integrity, family, freedom, creativity, compassion, or justice. Your purpose should align with your values.
- **Explore Interests:** Consider your hobbies, interests, and passions. Explore new activities and experiences to expand your horizons. Sometimes, your purpose emerges from something you're yet to discover.
- **Connect the Dots:** Analyze your answers to the reflection questions and look for common threads, patterns, and connections. Your purpose often emerges when you recognize a common theme in your life experiences and interests.
- **Seek Feedback:** Talk to friends, family, and mentors. They may offer insights into your strengths and qualities that you may not see in yourself.

- **Set Goals and Experiment:** Define specific, achievable goals related to your potential purpose. Start small experiments and projects that align with your emerging purpose. This can help you test and refine your ideas.
- **Embrace Change:** Be open to the possibility that your purpose can evolve or change over time. It's not a fixed destination, but a journey of self-discovery.

Remember that finding your why and purpose can take time and may not happen overnight. Be patient with yourself and enjoy the journey of self-discovery. Keep revisiting and refining your purpose as you learn and grow in life.

Ted Lasso gave a locker room speech to his team about belief and where it comes from. He gestured to his heart and stomach, indicating we need to listen to our heart and intuition, and followed it by saying, "The only problem is we've got so much junk floatin' around in here we can't even hear it." This is so true! Use Ted Lasso's speech as a reminder that you are a junk sifter. You get to decide what junk you allow to stay floating around in you, obstructing your ability to see your greatness. When things get challenging, you can call up your "why," your purpose, and what you are passionate about and realign yourself so that you will have the drive to push through the discomfort that growth requires.

REFLECTION QUESTIONS

Discovering your "why" and your life's purpose is a deeply personal and introspective journey. It involves self-reflection, exploration, and a willingness to ask and answer some challenging questions. Here's a step-by-step guide to help you find your why and purpose.

1. What activities or moments in your life bring you the most joy and fulfillment?

2. What are your natural talents, skills, and strengths?
3. What do others praise you for?
4. What are your values and principles?
5. What is truly important to you?
6. When have you felt most alive and in your element?
7. What are the common themes or recurring interests in your life, even from a young age?
8. What problems or issues in the world do you feel deeply passionate about solving?
9. Who are your role models or people you admire, and what qualities do they possess that resonate with you?
10. What would you do if you had all the time and resources in the world?
11. If you could make a positive impact on the world, what would it be?
12. What do you want to be remembered for?
13. What are the moments in life when you felt most in tune with your true self?
14. What do you believe is your unique contribution to the world?
15. What problem do you feel deeply compelled to help solve?
16. What makes you come alive? What energizes you?

ACTION STEP: DISCOVER YOUR MENTORS TO CONNECT WITH YOUR PASSION

- Write a list of six people you consider as your mentors and what you love about them.
- Connect what you like about these mentors to qualities that you already have and write them down.

- Write your mentors in the diagram below.

MY MENTORS

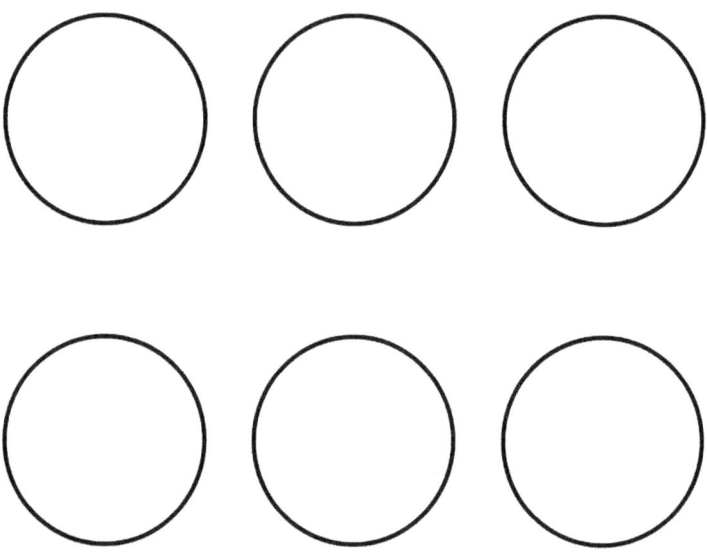

- Create a visual with their faces on it and hang it up where you can have it as a daily reminder.
- **Find Your Why:** Ask several of your close friends why they are friends with you. What gives you goosebumps from their responses?

- Fill in the blank ikigai diagram below with what you love, what you are good at, what you can be paid for, and what the world needs.

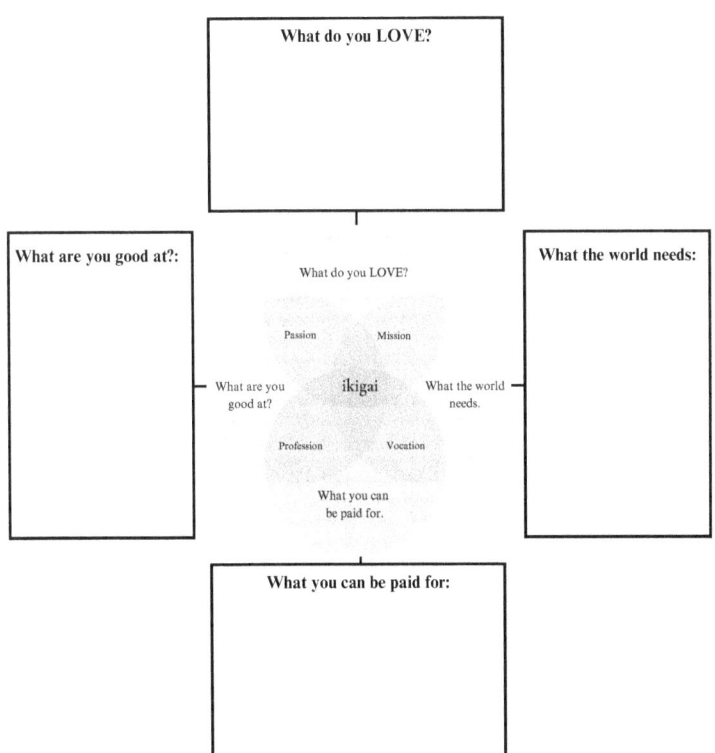

CHAPTER 11

READY, SET, GO!

Twenty percent of our actions get 80 percent of our results.
Tony Robbins

I t's been weeks since I opened my computer to write. I've been struggling with the hard conversations I need to have to finish this book and the general resistance I've been feeling to opening my document and completing it. I spoke with my writing coach this morning and shared everything I'm stuck on. I am afraid to ask people to include their story as it relates to mine in the book; I am worried about how others will receive my book if I must talk about it and how I will communicate the ideas I've presented in the book, and I am finding lots of distractions and things to do other than writing.

My coach said, "This may not be helpful because this is how I do things, but I just jump in!"

I immediately thought of the previous weekend at Lake Shasta on our family vacation, where I pushed myself to jump from the second story of our houseboat. I told myself not to think about it. Recently, we went to Croatia, and my husband did a cliff jump. I watched from the kayak. It was around a fifty-foot jump. When I asked him how it was, he replied, "It was good; it was very high!"

He proceeded to tell me that the guy going before him said, "Fear and overthinking are a universal language." He told my husband that the best way to overcome it is to not think about the fear and just jump. He then quickly added, "Uh oh, now I'm thinking about it!"

My husband laughed as he told me the story, but I will say that this is something he's trained himself well to do. He doesn't think too much before trying something, or else he would never do it. I'm the one who overthinks. There is a delicate balance here because I encourage my clients to think and process their emotions and work on their goals and clarity by thinking it through. But once you've set your goals and determined your direction, it's good to learn how and when to turn the overthinking off, calculate your risks, and then just jump!

Once we have our eye on the target, we can begin creating a list of actions we can take to get there. This is just a giant free brainstorming list. If, according to Tony Robbins, 80 percent of our outcomes result from 20 percent of our actions, then we don't even have to do *all the things*. However, a great cure for anxiety is to get it all out of our head and on paper so that we can evaluate, prioritize, and determine who can help us, or as Tony Robbins calls it, "Find leverage for as many actions as possible."

Especially if you are a go-getter, finding leverage can be a lifesaver. When I created the show *Fastlife*, I produced, edited, shot, wrote, and created the show. I reverted to my childhood declaration: "I can do it all by myself." My parents used to tell me that was my favorite phrase as a really young child. We are not designed to do it all by ourselves. We are social creatures, and when we rely on others to help us, it can increase our productivity or help us get through hard things. In her book *Unfiltered: No Shame, No Regrets, Just Me*, Lily

Collins said, "Asking for help is never a sign of weakness. It's one of the bravest things you can do. And it can save your life."[35] An actress and author, Collins has been open about her personal struggles with mental health and an eating disorder. She likely made the statement "asking for help can save your life" based on her own experiences and the importance of seeking support when facing difficult circumstances. I can resonate with this, being someone who didn't really ask for help well.

TIME TO GET COMFORTABLE OUTSIDE YOUR COMFORT ZONE

Get comfortable outside your comfort zone. Have fun!
Be wild!
Iris Apfel

When my husband Derek shared with me that he wanted to be a race car driver, my next question was, "Okay, what does it take to do that?" I went to the library to find books for him on famous drivers and their stories. There were very few at the time, but we found what was available, and he began reading. He also knew who the players were in the industry from passionately following the racing greats he loved and the sport in general. Aside from reading and studying what others had done, he needed to get out there and take some steps to begin learning. So, we signed him up for Skip Barber Racing School in California. We took a road trip down there with our young daughters, who were still in diapers at the time, and got him going and on a path to learning how to do the thing he was dreaming of.

---

35   Lily Collins, *Unfiltered: No Shame, No Regrets, Just Me* (London: Ebury Press, 2018).

Once you know what your target is, you can research the steps and work backward from the goal to create a reverse-engineered action plan.

REVERSE ENGINEERING AN ACTION PLAN

Creating a reverse-engineered action plan is a strategic approach to turning your dream into a reality. Here are the steps to craft such a plan:

- **Start with the End Goal:** Clearly define your dream goal. What does success look like? Understand the specific outcome you want to achieve.
- **Identify Milestones:** Break down your goal into smaller, manageable milestones or significant checkpoints. These intermediate goals will serve as progress markers along the way.
- **Set Deadlines:** Assign realistic deadlines to each milestone. This creates a sense of urgency and accountability, ensuring steady progress.
- **Work Backward:** Reverse-engineer the process by starting from your final milestone and working backward. Determine the steps necessary to reach each milestone.
- **Prioritize Tasks:** Organize your tasks in order of priority and dependency. Some steps may need to be completed before others can begin.
- **Detail Each Step:** For each task, outline the specific actions, resources, and skills required to complete it. Be as detailed as possible.
- **Allocate Resources:** Identify the resources, whether it's time, money, or personnel, needed for each step. Ensure you have access to what's required.
- **Build a Timeline:** Create a timeline or project plan that outlines when each task should be completed based on the reverse-engineered order.

- **Set Accountability Measures:** Define how you will track your progress and who will hold you accountable. This can be a mentor, coach, or yourself.
- **Adapt and Adjust:** As you implement your plan, be flexible and willing to adjust it as needed. Life can be unpredictable, and adapting is part of the process.
- **Stay Motivated:** Regularly revisit your dream goal, reminding yourself of the end vision to stay motivated and committed to your action plan.

By following these steps, you can develop a well-structured, reverse-engineered action plan that brings you closer to achieving your dream goal systematically and efficiently.

ANTICIPATE RESISTANCE

When I feel stuck, I always pray, even if the prayer is just, "God, help me!" I also think of a favorite passage from the Bible, "Lead me in paths of righteousness for his name's sake" (Psalm 23:3). "Show me the way," I will often say. This morning, that was the prayer, and here is the answer I got!

I was doing some research and was led to many websites with very helpful information about epigenetic trauma, which you've already read about in earlier chapters. I was also led to a podcast to help a family member through a toxic relationship, which was on my mind and helped me realize my writing energy was being blocked by fears relating to my family member's struggle. The devil loves to pile it on us, so we can't pick out the "leading error" or the root cause of what needs to be healed. Confusion and overwhelm is the name of the game the devil plays. "Block that healing energy," just like blocking in football. Block the progress of the ball down the field and the team's ability to score and similarly keeping all the energy and momentum toward distraction and problems instead of toward healing!

As I began to get answers to every concern or stronghold that was blocking my writing and getting this message out to you, a post popped up on my Instagram feed:

"Sorry to interrupt your scrolling, but are you okay? Be honest…"

This one hit me hard. It shed light on the last few weeks of taking a step back from my coaching goals and the fears I had been encountering about it. It made me think about all the work I had put in and that I was allowing fear and distraction to prevent me from taking steps forward into the unknown. It helped me see that I was scared to put myself out there and not know the exact outcome or how my message would be received. It helped me hear something my coach had told me earlier that morning, which was, "This book is about your healing journey. Stay focused on that. Not everyone will like your book; not everyone will read it."

And I clearly heard God's voice say, "The people who need to hear your message will."

As I processed my feelings and where I was in my book journey, I remembered something I learned from Tony Robbins in one course I had taken.

Remember this: Anticipation is the ultimate power.
Losers react; leaders anticipate.
Tony Robbins

He teaches that if we anticipate and prepare for challenges, we can move through them easier and come up with solutions. I laughed when I remembered this and felt a little silly for being so thrown off course there for a bit. Within a few hours, I was writing and back on pace to finish up the book to deliver my message to you.

This is a great reminder to share with you that you are not alone, and we are all learning how to be better leaders and humans. Each day, if we are willing to do a little reflection work as we go and stay open to new ideas, we can learn.

Taking Action When You're Stuck

Taking action might include some fearful moments and working through being stuck. When you invite God into the process, it opens a channel of communication again to hear God speaking to you. I was listening to a pastor the other day tell a story, and he was talking about being in periods of drought where things are not going well, and we can't hear God talking to us. He said, "God is frequently silent but not indifferent." While I agree with the second part of that and know God is not indifferent, I don't wholly agree with the notion that God is frequently silent. I think sometimes God needs us to take the first step and to invite Him back into our process, and then we begin to hear Him in all sorts of ways, as I did after my conversation with my coach. I prayed and took steps to share with my coach, do a little research, and look for God to show up in my day and communicate to me what I needed to hear and which way to go. Then the answers started pouring in!

For each of you, prayer will look a little different. How you ask for God to come into your experience will become customized to the best way for you. If someone tries to tell you that there is "only one way" or "one prayer to say," question that! Think about all the different ways prayer and healing happened in the Bible. There are all kinds of different stories. When the woman with an infirmity for years touched Jesus' garment, He said, "Your faith hath made you whole."

She didn't say some long prayer to ask to be forgiven; she just touched His garment and had faith in his ability to heal.[36]

When Jesus was tempted by the devil, His prayer was to take a stand against Satan and command that he get behind Him.[37] For Saul, it was getting on his knees and being willing to change and become Paul, following the light.[38] Prayer is asking, having faith, and then taking action in your life. Moving forward will come with a willingness to change and having the courage to step into the new you, let go of your old ways, and not overthink the risks. Trust God will carry and protect you.

WHAT I'VE LEARNED

For so long, I had survived the bullying and abuse by holding it all in and being the strong one, so I believed I could do it all myself. I did successfully get the *Fastlife* series on Amazon Prime, but I was not healthy once I did. Physically, I was depleted, and my kids were taking on the energy in the home. It's okay to ask for help! Don't do what I did. You can still lead a project and work with others. I now believe that it is much better to do it this way because you can also leverage others' gifts and abilities to make the project even better than it would be with just your ideas.

WHAT YOU CAN DO

There is no one way to grow, no one way to God, no one way to heal, no one way to become all you can be, but there are steps you can take to help your healing process along and get clear about the direction you want to move into. Freedom is having the ability to grow and change into the person God

---

36   Luke 8:43–48.
37   Matthew 4:1–11, Mark 1:12–13, Luke 4:1–13.
38   Acts 9.

intended you to be and the person your heart is calling you to become.

Once you know your action items for a particular project or desire, you can connect with who you want to be. Essentially, you will decide who you want to become, and this will require closing the gap from where you are now to who you want to become.[39] Reverse engineering is the most effective way to accomplish this. You take your goals and the list of action items and research you have, and you begin constructing a plan, working backward to your goal. Tools I find helpful in this process are creating a vision board, a values list, the qualities you admire in mentors, an assessment of where you are and where you want to be (the gap), and linking this to the person and qualities you want to express.

I'd like to leave you with one of my favorite quotes about life:

> *Success in life depends upon persistent effort, upon the improvement of moments more than upon any other one thing. A great amount of time is consumed in talking nothing, doing nothing, and indecision as to what one should do. If one would be successful in the future, let him make the most of the present.*
> **Mary Baker Eddy**

Your healing journey begins now! Take it one step at a time, set the baggage down, unpack what you don't need, and take with you the helpful lessons. Your values, your strength derived from experience, and reaching out to your God in humility for guidance and direction will become your beacon of light to follow. You've got this! I love you! I believe in you!

---

39 The Pyramid of Mastery - Tony Robbins, accessed November 4, 2023, https://pages.tonyrobbins.com/rs/299-KII-331/images/UPW_PreEvent_Worksheet_English.pdf.

REFLECTION QUESTIONS

In the journey of personal growth and development, we often encounter resistance and moments of feeling stuck. These challenges can arise for various reasons, from fear of the unknown to the comfort of the status quo. However, it's essential to work through these obstacles to continue growing and evolving as individuals. This process of overcoming resistance and breaking through stagnation is a fundamental part of the human experience. So, how can we navigate this terrain? Let's explore some reflection questions to help us understand and address the resistance we encounter on our path to personal growth.

1. What are the specific areas or aspects of your life where you currently feel resistance or stagnation when it comes to personal growth?
2. What might be the underlying reasons for this resistance? Is it fear, self-doubt, external pressures, or something else?
3. How does your comfort zone contribute to the feeling of being stuck? What familiar patterns or routines are you holding onto?
4. What long-term goals and aspirations are you working toward, and how might overcoming resistance align with these objectives?
5. Can you identify any past experiences when you successfully pushed through resistance? What strategies or mindset shifts were effective in those situations?
6. Who can support you on this journey? Do you have mentors, friends, or resources that can provide guidance and encouragement as you work through resistance and growth challenges?
7. What practices or techniques, such as meditation, mindfulness, or goal setting, can you employ to cultivate resilience and perseverance in the face of resistance?

8. How can you reframe your perspective on resistance, viewing it as an opportunity for growth rather than a hindrance?

ACTION STEP: CREATE YOUR ACTION PLAN

Time to take action! Now that you've identified your why, purpose, and the resistance you sometimes feel, it's time to create an action plan. Doing this requires clarity of the result you want. Using your vision board, create the steps to reverse engineer your action plan. Just do it! No more excuses! Remember, you can both be who you are and who you are working on becoming at the same time.

Create Your Wheel of Life

As a life coach, I tell my clients to take all areas of their lives and evaluate where they are and where they want to go. When we have a visual way to see what the status of our life is, it can be very motivating to create a plan for improvement. The below tool is called the "Wheel of Life." Draw an indicator of how fulfilled you are in all categories. The narrower part is less, and the wider part is more. Then, when you are done rating each category, connect your lines and see what type of circle you have.

If it's all over the place, it will be important to not only work on more fulfillment in each area but also to find more balance between the different areas of life. The goal is not only to have each category filled up, but the connected areas should make a circle. Remember, you are a work in progress; don't rush it. This is just a tool to help you find clarity in the areas of life you are focusing on improving.

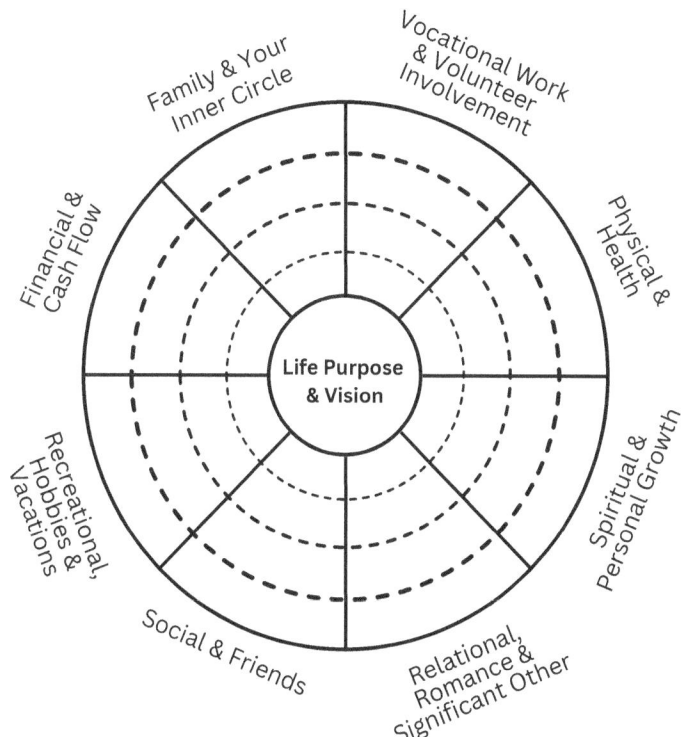

Create Your Action Plan (Identify the Gap)[40]

- Below you will find the tool to write out your dream life goals in each category that you assessed in the wheel of life. This will help you have the clarity you need about where you are, where you are headed, and the gap between the two. It also includes a checklist of suggestions about how you can close the gap. Clarity = Power!!!

---

40   The Pyramid of Mastery - Tony Robbins, accessed November 4, 2023, https://pages.tonyrobbins.com/rs/299-KII-331/images/UPW_PreEvent_Worksheet_English.pdf.

Choose three points of focus from your wheel of life:

Physical Body	Work/Career
Emotions & Meaning	Finances
Relationships	Celebrate/Contribute
Time	

1.

2.

3.

Describe your ideal life in those three areas:

What does your life feel like now?

What can you do to get closer to your goals?

- Post your vision board and action plan so you can see it daily. Get yourself a planner where you can write out your actions each week and write a paragraph in your journal as if you've already had a successful week about how that makes you feel.

POSTFACE:
NEXT STEPS

The courage to be vulnerable is not about winning or losing; it's about the courage to show up when you can't predict or control the outcome.
Brene Brown

'm hoping you are feeling more empowered and clearer about your tremendous value. You ARE valuable, and I believe with all my being that you were created to fulfill a very important purpose here in this lifetime. If you, like me, have been through experiences of bullying and abuse, you may have added extra baggage to your life that is weighing you down. The hope is that by setting that baggage down, opening it, and unpacking what you don't need, we've lightened your load so that you have the energy to go out and pursue your dreams. We need you to be the best, most empowered version of you! This is why I became a coach. After doing years of work and finally finding my way, all I want to do is help others do the same. So today is your day to say "Yes!" to you and "No" to denying your own power by pleasing people, staying in unhealthy, unsupportive relationships, having poor boundaries, and giving away your power! You are now prepared to put the baggage down and pick up the torch you are to carry and share your light with the world! Your part of the puzzle is getting added to the universal puzzle and will ultimately help the world be a happier place.

So, let's recap what we've learned! You are valuable and have a gift to share with the world. The number one thing that you now know is that a bit of self-awareness can go a long way. Getting clear on your values, boundaries, hopes, and dreams is super important to create an action plan to get to where you want to go and who you want to be. And, maybe even more important, is getting out of your own way. Over our lifetime, we accumulate experiences, and we develop feelings and stories about these experiences that live in us. Until we take the time to develop awareness about what those beliefs and stories are, it is difficult to be our best and likely keeps us stalled in a survival place rather than really thriving and growing. Hopefully, you have received some tools in this book to begin doing the work of removing the limiting beliefs and stepping into your power. If you feel that you would like extra support, you can reach out to me for coaching.

My prayer for you was given to me by a dear friend when I was in Sunday School:

May today there be peace within you.
May you not forget the infinite possibilities that are born of faith.
May you use those gifts that you have received
and pass on the love that has been given to you.
May you be content knowing that you are a child of God.
Let His presence settle into your bones,
And allow your soul the freedom to sing, dance,
And to bask in the sun.
It is there for each and every one of you.

Please stay connected and sign up today for my free newsletter and blog that covers everything discussed in this book, life tips, recommendations, and more! You can also get in touch with me to share your insights from the exercises in this book and apply for my Freelife Academy coaching program on my website:

www.thebrookedeboer.com

APPENDIX A
CORE VALUES

Authenticity
Achievement
Adventure
Authority
Autonomy
Balance
Beauty
Boldness
Compassion
Challenge
Citizenship
Community
Competency
Contribution
Creativity
Curiosity
Determination
Fairness
Faith
Fame
Friendships
Fun
Growth
Happiness
Honesty
Humor
Influence
Inner Harmony
Justice

Kindness
Knowledge
Leadership
Learning
Love
Loyalty
Meaningful Work
Openness
Optimism
Peace
Pleasure
Poise
Popularity
Recognition
Religion
Reputation
Respect
Responsibility
Security
Self-Respect
Service
Spirituality
Stability
Success
Status
Trustworthiness
Wealth
Wisdom

APPENDIX B
RESOURCES FOR
UNSAFE LIVING
ENVIRONMENTS

National Domestic Violence Hotline: 1-800-799-SAFE (1-800-799-7233) or visit their website at www.thehotline.org.

RAINN (Rape, Abuse & Incest National Network): 1-800-656-HOPE (1-800-656-4673) or visit their website at www.rainn.org.

Loveisrespect: Text "LOVEIS" to 22522 or call 1-866-331-9474. You can also visit their website at www.loveisrespect.org for help with dating and relationship abuse.

National Child Abuse Hotline: 1-800-4-A-CHILD (1-800-422-4453) or visit their website at www.childhelp.org.

National Suicide Prevention Lifeline: 1-800-273-TALK (1-800-273-8255) provides support for individuals in crisis.

Human Trafficking Hotline: 1-888-373-7888 or text "HELP" or "INFO" to 233733. You can also visit www.humantraffickinghotline.org.

National LGBTQ+ Anti-Violence Hotline: 1-212-714-1141 offers support to LGBTQ+ individuals experiencing violence or abuse.

The Trevor Project: 1-866-488-7386 provides crisis intervention and suicide prevention for LGBTQ+ youth.

National Runaway Safeline: 1-800-RUNAWAY (1-800-786-2929) offers help for youth thinking about running away or already on the streets.

Your Local Crisis Center: Many communities have local organizations and shelters for victims of domestic violence, abuse, and homelessness. You can search for local resources or shelters in your area for more specific assistance.

If you are in immediate danger, please call emergency services in your country (e.g., 911 in the United States) for immediate assistance. Remember, it's important to reach out for help if you're in an unsafe situation. You are not alone, and there are people and organizations ready to provide support and assistance.

ADDITIONAL RESOURCES

- **Values List by Brene Brown:**
  - o https://brenebrown.com/resources/dare-to-lead-list-of-values/
- **Attachment Styles:**
  - o https://psychcentral.com/health/4-attachment-styles-in-relationships
- **Attachment Styles in Relationships and How They Change:**
  - o https://www.psychologytoday.com/us/blog/the-mysteries-love/201502/attachment-styles-cant-change-can-they
- **Mount Sinai Adolescent Health Center:**
  - o https://teenhealthcare.org

READ THE INSPIRING CHILDREN'S BOOK:

FASTLIFE: LET'S GO RACING

Scan for more by
Brooke DeBoer

A book that supports kids to believe in themselves
and live their dreams!

BY: BROOKE DEBOER

Thank You for Reading

Living the FreeLife!

I really appreciate your feedback and love hearing what you have to say. Your input is valuable to me so that I can make the next version of this book and future books better.

Please take two minutes now to leave a review on Amazon letting me know what you thought of the book:

With Gratitude,

-Brooke DeBoer

For more helpful resources and reflection questions:

visit my website: www.thebrookedeboer.com/author

or

scan this QR code now!

ACKNOWLEDGMENTS

My heartfelt gratitude extends to a multitude of cherished individuals who have played profound roles in my journey. First and foremost, to my incredible husband, who has offered me unwavering support and a safe space to confront and heal from the trauma of the past. You've helped me rediscover self-love, growth, and the limitless potential within. To my three remarkable daughters, Paige, Haylee, and Ryann, your inspiring qualities continually fuel my aspirations. Paige's honesty and quirky humor, Haylee's immense heart and work ethic, and Ryann's unwavering self-assuredness and kindness brighten my life.

My parents, Rod and Nancy, your love and support have been steadfast, even during my challenging teenage years and beyond. Your commitment and resilience are the very essence of your love. My Aunt Susan, who escaped an abusive realtionship with her first husband and dedicated her life to her healing and shared with me along the way. I hold you dear as a second mom. Your enduring presence in my life has been a profound source of strength and inspiration. You've shown me that, as strong women, we possess the power to overcome any obstacle. Your incredible sense of fashion has not only adorned us in style but has also taught me to appreciate the art of self-expression. Thank you for your unwavering support adn the valuable lessons you imparted. You've played a remarkable role in shaping the person I am today.

A special thanks to Jennifer Ndalmia for mentoring me and providing valuable insights into both my Reiki training and coaching development. Ania, your unconditional love and unwavering kindness have meant the world to me. To my coaches, Noreen, Kevin, and my dear friend and coach

Louise, thank you for guiding me to my true self, and helping me shed the layers of life's challenges that dimmed my inner light. To JoAnn Boufis, for believing in my story and supporting me in getting my first book published.

To God, I'm eternally grateful for your constant presence, guidance, and protection, even when I turned a blind eye. Gene Carlisle and Gayle, thank you for planting the seeds of confidence and belief in me. Lu Crenshaw, your words empowered me to stop apologizing, and your training at Camp 17 (now Drop Gym), alongside Shantel, has been invaluable.

Dr. Delgado, your compassionate care during my health challenges meant the world to me. Marcia Durham, you've taught me the importance of treating myself as a masterpiece. My brother Spencer, your humor and adventurous spirit have been a lifelong inspiration.

To all my teachers, whose guidance and challenges helped me push beyond my limits. Melinda, you provided unwavering support during one of the darkest and most transformative periods of my life. To my dear friend Christy, thank you for seeing my heart and treating me with kindness. My racing family and friends, especially Violette and Beverly, have become my sisters, inspiring radical honesty and a deep love of God.

To all the friends and family I haven't mentioned by name, you remain cherished in my heart. Your presence has enriched my life in countless ways, and I carry you with me daily. Thank you for your invaluable role in my journey.

ABOUT THE AUTHOR

Brooke DeBoer is a dedicated advocate for personal transformation and self-discovery. Her core belief in the unique purpose of every individual, intricately designed by God to play a specific role in the grand puzzle of life, has driven her to inspire and empower others to overcome limiting beliefs and heal from the scars of trauma caused by abuse and bullying. As a compassionate life coach, she specializes in guiding women to find clarity in their purpose and equips them with actionable plans to manifest the lives of their dreams, serving as both a guide and an unwavering accountability partner.

Brooke's creative spirit shines through her work, with the creation of the captivating docuseries *Fastlife,* available on Amazon Prime from 2018 to 2023, and now on YouTube. The series chronicles her husband's journey to becoming a professional race car driver and the unwavering support their family provides.

In 2020, Brooke authored a heartwarming children's book called *Fastlife: Let's Go Racing,* teaming up with her daughter Paige, who created the original conceptual illustrations, about their shared journey to chase their dreams—him as a race car driver and Brooke as a photographer and filmmaker. Through her endeavors, Brooke seeks to inspire courage, limitless thinking, and the pursuit of audacious dreams. She firmly believes that life's experiences are valuable lessons rather than failures, and she is on a mission to provide others with the tools to rebuild their lives by conquering trauma, shame, and self-imposed limitations.

With a profound love for her husband, Derek, and their three beautiful daughters, animals and nature, a deep desire to explore the world, and a passion for spreading happiness, Brooke aims to create a brighter, more joyful world. Trained in Level One Reiki, she nurtures her spiritual connection and a thirst for life's adventures.